The Great Escape

Your guide to early retirement
and financial freedom

The Great Escape

Your guide to early retirement
and financial freedom

John White

The McGraw-Hill Companies

London   Burr Ridge, IL   New York   St Louis   San Francisco   Auckland   Bogotá
Caracas   Lisbon   Madrid   Mexico   Milan   Montreal   New Delhi   Panama   Paris
San Juan   São Paulo   Singapore   Sydney   Tokyo   Toronto

Published by
McGraw-Hill Professional
Shoppenhangers Road, Maidenhead, Berkshire, SL6 2QL
Telephone: 44 (0) 1628 502 500
Fax: 44 (0) 1628 770 224
Website: www.mcgraw-hill.co.uk

British Library Cataloguing in Publication Data
A catalogue record for this book is available from the British Library

Library of Congress Cataloguing in Publication Data
The Library of Congress data for this book is available from the Library of Congress

Sponsoring Editor: Elizabeth Robinson
Editorial Assistant: Sarah Wilks
Production Editorial Manager: Penny Grose
Desk Editor: Alastair Lindsay

Produced for McGraw-Hill by Steven Gardiner Ltd
Printed and bound by Bell & Bain Ltd, Glasgow
Cover design by Senate Design Ltd

McGraw-Hill

A Division of The McGraw·Hill Companies

ISBN 0 07 709841 2

McGraw-Hill books are available at special quantity discounts. Please contact the
Corporate Sales Executive at the above address.

*For my family
and all of my past students
and in loving memory of
Archie Willey and Bill Bayton*

Contents

Contents

About the author

John White took early retirement in 1994, after a 30-year stint in education, much of it spent as a lecturer in English and Journalism at the North Oxfordshire College, Banbury. A sabbatical year, given for study for a master's degree, involved so much enjoyable writing that, in 1982, he resolved to become a part-time sports journalist. Eight years later, he became the first and only freelance ever to be voted Magazine Sportswriter of the Year.

The author of five sports books – one a complete *Racegoers' Encyclopaedia* – he began *The Great Escape* when he realised that, whilst many books had been written on statutory retirement at 65, very little had ever been produced for the early leaver.

The Chief Examiner in literacy for the AQA Examining Board, he lives in the West Country.

Acknowledgements

My first debt is to Terry Williams, the author of a succinct article on early retirement that appeared in the journal of my lecturers' union in the 1990s. He set me thinking and 'tunnelling' so as to achieve my own 'Great Escape'!

The war film of this name provided many fruitful images and much inspiration, as did, sometimes unwittingly, several former colleagues at the North Oxfordshire College in Banbury, where, prior to my early retirement, I spent the greatest proportion of my working life.

Many recent articles in and supplements to the *Daily Telegraph*, *The Times*, *What Investment* and *Personal Finance* have proved valuable sources of reference. However, for financial advice, information and guidance, my greatest debt by far is to Peter Hargreaves, the author or producer of a number of Hargreaves Lansdown publications on many subjects relevant to early leaving. Peter's generous support, encouragement, and advice have been greatly appreciated and have done much to smooth the passage of this book into print.

Another who made the birth of this book a far easier affair is my sponsoring editor at McGraw-Hill, Elizabeth Robinson, whose sensitivity and dynamism I have found so welcome and refreshing.

Finally, I have to thank my long-suffering wife Dorothy for her unflagging faith in me and all my works.

Introduction

As the twenty-first century progresses, several once well-established and frequently repeated patterns of employment are fading rapidly. One such pattern – the 'gold watch' syndrome of retiring at 65 from a working life of forty or more years spent in one job or field of employment – has given way in the hard-nosed, market-led, short-term, 'contract culture' of the new millennium to a new situation where the average age of those retiring is only 55!

Of course, some of these early leavers have this experience thrust upon them through being made redundant compulsorily. But there are many thousands who, not just for their sustenance, but also to sustain the lifestyles they desire, choose to end their dependency on the salaries they have so long received. It is to this ever-growing group and the many thousands of others affected by early (and later) retirement that this book is addressed and dedicated.

That early retirement is both an actuality for the majority and an aspiration of millions more is confirmed both by the fact that eight out of ten who leave Britain's largest companies do so prematurely, and the findings of a Barclays bank survey that 68 per cent of its customers want to retire early.

Despite the Government's plans to discourage really early retirement, before the age of 55, this actuality and aspiration are both unlikely to change. Rather, it seems pretty certain that retirement will continue to be taken early and, with medical advances, to last even longer as 'life's longest holiday'. However, financing it to levels of prosperity well beyond mere subsistence will increasingly and heavily devolve on the individual, especially as the value of state support in retirement is likely to dwindle even more drastically.

It is estimated that within a decade the over 50s will make up four out of ten of our population. This will give the 'grey empowered' the electoral clout to get many of its demands satisfied – for example, demands for more flexible retirement arrangements and for more choice about how, when and where they can work (or not to). Further, it is noteworthy that some of the recently launched stakeholder pensions have been marketed with such blandishments as 'the sooner you start, the sooner you could stop working'. These new pension plans should help many, and increasingly younger, prospective early leavers to shore up the sides of their 'Great Escape' tunnels.

So there has never been a better time for a practical and inspirational guide to early (and later) retirement. If you number yourself amongst the ever-growing group who:

- are dreaming of early retirement
- wondering whether to take it
- planning for it
- actually applying for it
- being offered/offering it
- accepting it
- experiencing it,

or are one of those many thousands of others indirectly affected by what is a major life-changing experience, this book is for YOU!

Whatever your situation, it is important to recognise the very considerable difference between 'statutory' retirement in your 60s and early leaving which many experience around the age of 55. First, the very word 'statutory' means that retirement is a legal requirement and thus something those involved are obliged to experience, while early leaving is usually a voluntary or semi-voluntary affair – a matter or object of desire, personal preference and choice. Less commonly, because of redundancy or ill-health, it is an obligation.

Not that 'jumping ship' (while some of one's contemporaries remain at sea for many more years) is likely to be free of hazard. Indeed, one problem is that those who retire at 55 may well risk reducing the 'works' pension they would otherwise have received on 'full' retirement by 40 per cent. However, this loss of eventual pension power will prove this substantial only as regards their occupational pension arrangements. It constitutes a shortfall that can, at the very least, be readily made up, because early leavers have at their disposal hour upon hour of uncommitted time in which to earn and invest further sums.

The words 'at the very least' are crucial here. Many of those taking early retirement tend to be so intrepid, energetic and dynamically self-directing that (especially since their severance lump sums are often invested to provide further income) they end up rather better off than when they were employed full time. In general, many who retire early, rather than as late as is allowed, are likely to be fitter, more energetic, healthier and stronger, and thus far better equipped to cope with the major sea change that giving up full-time employment always involves.

Early leavers are still relatively young, yet very experienced. They are probably far better off than when they were young workers building up their careers, setting up homes and bringing up families. After giving up their 'day jobs', many who retire early are ideally placed to re-invent themselves and re-direct the course of the many years commonly left to them. They are far more likely than traditional 'statutory' retirees to feel they have a good deal left to contribute and achieve. Moreover, the lesser likelihood they have been written off as spent forces who have been unproductively 'put out to grass' also means they are more likely to see themselves in a positive and dynamic light.

What is more, their severance lump sums will give many early leavers more money to lodge in income- and growth-producing investments than may have been available to them in their harder, earlier years. If their nests are empty of expensive-to-keep children, they may well find they have even more money to dispose of in self-fulfilling and self-indulgent ways than when they were hedonistic young adults. Because, too, they are likely to be more vital and less drained than 'statutory' retirees (who, admittedly, may get bus passes and other perks, and do get the rather niggardly State retirement pension), early leavers are far better equipped to engage in the adventurous, varied and physically quite demanding activities that, significantly, the Saga organisation now markets to the large 'grey-empowered' group of our population who are over 50.

WARNING

Stock market investments, including gilt and loan stocks, unit trusts, investment trusts, insurance products, property and alternative investments, can go down in value as well as up. The income from most securities can be subject to such movement. When you seek financial advice, ask about marketability.

The investments referred to in the following pages are for illustrative purposes only. You should not regard yourself as invited to purchase them, because that is always a matter on which advice about your particular circumstances should always be sought.

Neither the publisher nor the author accept any legal responsibility for the contents of this book, which is not intended to be a substitute for detailed professional advice taking into account individual readers' particular financial situations, needs and desires. Readers should conduct their own investment activity through an appropriately authorised individual or concern.

SECTION ONE

Digging the tunnel – vital preliminaries

As a truly Great Escape, early retirement is such an enticing, though far from simply achieved, experience that its success depends on several *vital preliminaries*. The first is covered in Chapter One and involves asking the all-important question 'why take premature retirement?', and then recognising that the fears and misgivings that should be felt when it is answered (covered in Chapter Two) need not be too daunting. Planning, as explained in Chapter Three, is the most important prerequisite for early leaving and a vital part of this is explained in Chapter Four. This involves weighing up your future entitlements to any occupational, private and (reduced) State pension, and to any other sources of cash or income. Chapter Five deals with costing-out your likely post-retirement expenditure and income, while Chapter Six looks at the timing of your escape and the financial shoring up of the sides of the tunnel through which you can make it.

1

Why premature retirement?

How full of briars is this working-day world
As you Like It, Act I

OVERVIEW

Have you noticed that many who take early retirement do so for very positive, if varied, reasons? You may wish to give up your 'day job' to achieve a long-held ambition, or to become self-employed instead of remaining on a payroll. Perhaps you want to do work that is more fulfilling, creative or philanthropic, or to spend more of your time in pleasurable activities, in sporting or leisure pursuits, or to take more frequent, longer or more exotic holidays. You may see your early leaving as a passport to a less-constrained lifestyle, or want to give up your work because it drains, displeases or dissatisfies you, or fails to bring any fulfilment. You could even find that financially you have no need to continue to earn your living!

Why premature retirement?

Were this question 'why retire?' it would be possible to give a much shorter answer, since the reasons why those of 'statutory' retirement age give up their jobs are well known and fairly self-evident. But if the words 'premature' and 'retirement' are featured in the question then the answers that can be given are much more varied, far less obvious and of rather more interest.

In many respects this is because of the inappropriateness of both the words 'premature' and 'retirement'. After all, the former has connotations of the untimely, the possibly problematic and the unprepared for, whilst the latter suggests withdrawal and a cessation of activity. Ironically, such notions bear little relation to the aspirations and fulfilling involvements of many who give up their jobs before they are obliged to. These individuals see this development in their lives as not premature, but opportune, one that allows them a chance to try out enticing new experiences or to savour those that their previous work has often precluded, marginalised or cut short. Such a revitalisingly different and fresh deployment of the time, talents and energies of these very positively inclined early leavers often reflects the fact that they see early retirement as a liberating force that accords them the freedom and the time to do the things they would prefer to do.

Some of those who see early retirement in this very positive light may, when they experience it, try to achieve a long-held (and possibly long-repressed) ambition that has been burning away within them but remained unfulfilled because of the constraints of their full-time employment. One early leaver whose decision to leave lecturing early was influenced by illness felt so well after retiring that he embarked on a series of marathon cycle rides right across several continents!

In some cases a desire to fulfil and live out through early retirement a long-cherished dream may involve a change of role as an employee or, more radically, entrepreneurial activity or self-employment of some kind. This is understandable, because some severance packages are sufficiently sizeable as to provide what may be seen as 'surplus' capital that is ideally suited to the funding of business ventures.

Thus guest houses are purchased, franchises obtained and businesses involving varying products and services established. My own father-in-law, for example, very soon after taking early retirement, set up a haulage business – before he'd actually passed his HGV driving test. He had such a vested interest in passing his test that when he did so, he took £100 from his lump sum and in gratitude gave it to his startled instructor!

Alternatively, some may wish to say goodbye to their full-time work so they can engage in some form of creative or philanthropic endeavour, whether or not this is undertaken to produce an income. Their overriding aim here is to find fulfilment by operating on some plane out of reach of what Oscar Wilde would have seen as the 'trammelling limitations' of their past employment.

Again, some give up their work prematurely so as to commence or extend their participation in pleasurable pastimes, sports, hobbies, interests or pursuits, while others may covet the chance to rest, relax, or go on holidays, taken when they wish.

Then there are those sybarites or hedonists who, in the true spirit of football polls fantasists or would-be Lottery winners, see early retirement as making possible one long unimpeded round of pleasurable self-indulgence!

Others who see early retirement as giving them freedom, not just from familiar employment, but also the freedom to do something with which they wish to become familiar, may yearn to engage in activity that is radically different from what they have long done as workers. Indeed, some applicants for premature retirement may wish to shatter, rather than merely break, the mould of their habitual employment. They may well be strongly motivated by a desire to experience activities and lifestyles that are far less constrained, conventional, complex, and even 'respectable' than those their past work has involved them in. Some, like the French painter Paul Gaugin, may feel this desire can only be satisfied by a physical escape to a less well developed part of the world where a simpler and more congenial lifestyle prevails. Somerset Maugham's tale of a British bank manager who, like many taking early retirement, 'drops out' (in his case by becoming something of a 'lotus eater' on a Mediterranean island) is all about such a yearning.

Interestingly, it was such a desire that recently drove one particular 'dark horse' of an early leaver I worked with in land-locked Banbury to retire early so he could transform a hovel he'd bought on the Greek island of Paxos into a base for for his idyll! Perhaps, like fellow escapee Shirley Valentine, he realised that when involved with the common round and daily task of our working role all too often 'we don't do what we want to, but what we feel we have to do – and then pretend it's what we want to do'.

Whilst a literal, truly terrestrial, broadening of his horizons was sought by 'Paxos man', this may be pursued in less spectacular ways. Some may relocate permanently within this country, or temporarily give up their daily journey to work so they can travel much more extensively.

More unusually, some want to leave a particular field of employment in which they have achieved a good deal because they feel there is little more they can achieve in it that they would value. Very familiar, since often repeated, satisfactions can lose their attraction to highly competent but restless practitioners. One of these, film actor Richard Dreyfus, perhaps out of a wish to get out while at the top, lost his desire to act and stopped doing so at the peak of his powers after he'd won an Oscar. Another consummate performer, pop singer Cat Stevens, turned his back on fortune and fame for the unworldly sake of his Islamic faith.

Of course, not all early leavers give up their jobs for predominantly positive reasons. Indeed, such are the pressures and constraints of many contemporary forms of employment that it is no wonder that millions yearn to free themselves from them. Revealingly, one recent commentator on working patterns in Japan made the comment that some jobs for life, i.e. those held until statutory retirement age, 'lock workers in but don't lock misery out'. Such misery in employment, of which the monstrous and detestably servile Caliban complained in *The Tempest*, can be so acute that, like parole, early retirement may be seen as a welcome way of cutting short a long sentence to an unpleasant way of spending time.

Indeed, many to whom early retirement appeals desire to be released from their work because of what it entails or causes them to feel or experience. While some may seek a literal physical escape from an imprisoning workplace (like that of 'Matthew and Son', bemoaned by Cat Stevens before he gave up singing about it), many more seek a metaphorical one, from heavy workloads, long or unsocial hours or other unappealing working conditions, and see early leaving as a way of saying goodbye to such unwanted feelings as disenchantment, disillusionment, disappointment, frustration, boredom, tedium, drudgery, stress, anxiety, worry, servitude, servility, exhaustion, exploitation, poor prospects, and little or no recognition of their worth!

Since many middle-aged employees, to whom the carrot of early retirement is increasingly being offered, have for most of their careers been used to contracts designed to protect their rights and working conditions, it is understandable that many should seek deliverance from the dubious ministrations of a new breed of confrontational managers whose priorities have more to do with getting more for less than with any promotion of employees' interests. Indeed, many prospective early leavers who have given a great deal by way of committed service over many years are surely entitled to feel that many aggressive modern-day managers do not deserve their services!

In the case of many middle-aged and long-serving employees, such feelings have been exacerbated by such effluvia of the presently rampant market culture as bullying managements with their Neanderthal approaches to trade unions. No wonder then that many such employees are currently contemplating getting out of working 'kitchens', in which the heat has been turned up to what they regard as unbearable levels by uncaring managers and in which they find themselves under such pressure.

Some experienced workers also feel that both they and their work have suffered a devaluation they are no longer prepared to stomach. If for most of their working lives they have had served up to them a much more wholesome, far richer and healthier 'diet' of much better resourced and palatable occupational experience, rather understandably, they may not relish dining off thinner fare.

Some, of course, apply for premature retirement for fortunate or fortuitous reasons. A sizeable capital gain, perhaps through an inheritance, along with or without a severance lump sum, may absolve its recipient from the need to continue in full-time employment, whilst the loss of a loved one may reduce or remove the need or the desire of a worker eligible for premature retirement to remain on a payroll.

KEY ADVICE

■ Remember there are many compelling reasons for early retirement.

■ Try to assess how relevant and pressing these are to you.

- Ask yourself 'how' you might retire early, as well as 'why'. Remember, this life-enhancing opportunity may well come in late middle age and via an offer that may not be made for long.
- Consider the case histories of early leavers you know and of the individuals mentioned in this chapter.
- Take comfort in the fact that you are far from alone in your aspirations regarding early retirement, since the average age of those retiring is well under 60.
- Prepare to subject the reasons why you might retire to some healthy scepticism, which is coming your way in the next chapter!

2
Facing up to fears and anxieties

Show boldness and aspiring confidence
King John, Act I

OVERVIEW

If you take seriously the prospect of any offer of early retirement, it is likely and appropriate that, as well as feelings of excitement, your immediate responses will include some fears and anxieties. These may involve worries about the onset of boredom and the undermining of your sense of identity through losing the feeling of self-worth that performing your occupational role has brought you. You may feel misgivings about losing skills if these are no longer exercised and giving up the security that comes with 'knowing the ropes' of your work. You may have fears that you will miss the companionship of colleagues and that some of these may see you as a 'quitter' who could not stand the heat or keep up the pace. You may wonder how you will cope when the 'strings' controlling you as a working 'puppet' are removed and you no longer receive the pay cheque you've been used to. You may also fear that ageist prejudice and the stigma of redundancy may jeopardise your chances of securing some replacement income through new employment.

It is inevitable and right that you feel such fears. But these are often exaggerated and can be allayed if early retirement is the sequel to proper planning and taken in the dauntless spirit of so many military stategists and successful escapees.

Premature retirement brings with it the prospect of such a major 'sea change' in circumstances, lifestyle, identity, and role that it is no wonder those contemplating it experience many misgivings. The point about these is, whilst often exaggerated, they ought to be experienced. For what early leaving really represents is the cutting away of familiar ground from beneath your feet, which naturally makes you uncertain of where you may stand in future.

When, in *Henry I, Part One*, Shakespeare commented that,

> *If all the year were playing holidays,*
> *To sport would be as tedious as to work*

he expressed, in his inimitable style and phrasing, the belief that prolonged respite from work might prove as irksome as its performance. This particular concern is just one of several fears and major misgivings that can dissuade many who have been conditioned by the common round or daily grind of long-established full-time employment from abandoning it through premature retirement.

Another is the very real fear that the removal, via a financially acceptable severance package, of the need to work may also bring about an erosion of notions of self-worth that the performance of this work has done much to establish. To a prospective early leaver, what answer to give in future when asked about your employment seems as daunting as the fear of becoming, as far as work is concerned, something of a yesterday's man or woman.

Anxieties that we may not be able to occupy ourselves in sufficiently satisfying ways, that we may not be able to acquire new interests and activities to fill the many unassigned hours we will have at our disposal, that we will find time hanging heavily on our hands and that we will eventually grow tired of such home-based activities as DIY, gardening and car maintenance may also persuade some employees they'd best take 'proper', rather than early, retirement.

Another very real anxiety of many who contemplate, or have to accept, premature retirement is that the particular physical or intellectual capacities called for in our work may be lost or impaired if we stop performing this work. Many, along with Hamlet, may feel guilty about spending time in unproductive inactivity. Some may even regard any future failure on their part to exercise their faculties and capacities (to the full or large extent that the performance of their regular jobs called for) as reprehensible and reductive of their very humanity. Like Hamlet, they might ask the question: 'what is a man, if his chief good and market of his time be but to sleep and feed?' Such concern about degenerating into debilitating and merely animal physicality is, of course, in line with both the Protestant work ethic and the truism about losing what you no longer use. Doubtless they do much to dissuade many from living the life of Riley in early retirement. In their most extreme form they may lie behind the case histories of those of full pensionable age who, shortly after retirement in their sixties, have become pale shadows of their former working selves, or have even died – through the removal of an important part of their raison d'être. The words 'raison d'être' are significant because some prospective retirees may have savoured feeling especially important or valuable as a result of carrying out their occupational duties and may have prized the reputations they have gained for the excellence of their work. No surprise then that they wonder whether they should give up work that has brought them fulfilment and made them feel worthwhile and therefore good about themselves.

Mention has already been made of the traditional Protestant work ethic, which is still operative today, if the words 'idleness brings disgrace' that appear on a currently available tea towel are anything to go by! Interestingly, the sheer power and pervasiveness of this belief are such that some potential early leavers may be dissuaded from giving up their jobs before they are required to. This is unfortunate, if not ironic, because idleness is seldom experienced by those who retire at any stage of their lives. After all, how many times have the retired been heard observing in the light of their busy lives that they do not know how they ever found time to go to work?

The questions 'what happens now? . . .where am I going to?', part of the lyrics of the popular song by Andrew Lloyd-Webber, give precise expression to another misgiving relating to coping with change that can beset those considering or facing early retirement. This is the fear of entering the 'undiscovered country' and the unknown experiences that await them if they venture beyond the familiar territory of the home ground of their full-time employment.

Fears about a new life they don't yet know may incline some not to chance this venture.

In the case of some prospective early leavers, the question marks they see around their futures may put a full stop to any thoughts of ending their present work, even if this involves unappealing elements or irksome demands and constraints they have found difficult to cope with. Indeed, some with the option of early retirement are like the soldier-on-leave hero of an American short story. He had long performed not always pleasant work that called for discipline and determination. This stretched him to the limit of his will, strength and capabilities, but he feared its abandonment would bring about his rapid degeneration. The soldier in question was so conditioned by the demanding daily tasks he had to perform when on duty that he found the prospect of never going back to his unit and so having to be fully in control of his destiny very disconcerting. Indeed, after finding prolonged inactivity on leave had a paralysing effect on him and that it made him moody and depressed, he longed for his leave to be over. Then he could once again feel secure and worthwhile through carrying out, within a rigidly structured organisational framework, an occupational role that he did not personally have to determine. Thus he avoided the collapse he feared he would suffer if the strings supporting him as a working 'puppet' were removed and he had to dance to his own working tune.

Such collapses are by no means rare amongst those who cease to perform rigorously structured roles that feature a good deal of routine. For example, sadly but significantly, a large number of servicemen, after years of falling-in on the parade ground, drop down and out when in civvy street they find themselves jobless.

Another misgiving about giving up your regular work may involve forfeiting the company of colleagues. The fact that many romances blossom and flourish at workplaces is just one reminder of the variety and depth of relationships that can develop between employees. If potential retirees have, as is often the case, shared a good deal of their lives with certain colleagues and feel these individuals have done much to enrich their lives, then quite understandably they may have misgivings about receiving goodbye cards! If they see themselves as valued members of well-established working teams, prospective retirees may loathe being left out of workplace scripts in which they have played appreciated, if not always starring, roles. To be told by those you plan to leave behind that your departure from a workplace would represent a 'great loss' may be flattering, but it may also cause you to reflect that in future the loss to you of the company of colleagues you esteem may be acutely felt. Thus a prospective retiree could be deterred by fear of living a rather lonelier life in future and of proving unable to find friends in other workplaces or elsewhere to replace those left behind on retirement.

Fear of being adjudged a 'quitter', of being seen as someone who was unable to last the full course of working life, who pulled up short before the finishing line of full-time employment, let alone the 'unsaddling enclosure', was reached, may also deter some from leaving work before they need to do so. I once arranged for my 'early retirement' from an agonising race during my school's sports day by getting my twin brother to trip me up well before its last lap. Now, forty years later, I still feel the shame of this!

Naturally, one of the greatest misgivings about no longer performing your habitual working role involves the belief that, as a consequence, your income will fall to an unacceptably low level, especially if you are in late middle age and fearful of being rejected as too old for employment. In many cases, however, this fear may be greatly exaggerated, as the loss of your 'milk cheque' will be compensated by the acquisition of hour upon hour of time in which you can earn sums to supplement your severance package – sometimes to such an extent that you may end up better off than when employed full time! Moreover, skilful investment of retirement lump sums and removal of the need to meet expenses connected with your previous employment – such as National Insurance contributions and travelling costs – may do much to dispel financial worries that may be clouding the prospect of a happy early retirement and mean that your actual disposable income as an early leaver is much higher than you initially calculated.

Another source of guilt and worry to prospective early leavers is the effects of what they are contemplating or accepting on those close to them – spouses, partners, children, friends and relatives. Retirement can come so early in some workers' lives that the radical changes it promises may appear likely to have undesirable repercussions on the lives of those to whom they are attached. When I was first offered early retirement, I eventually decided not to accept it because the relocation it would have involved would have had unacceptable effects on my daughter, who at that time still had a crucial final year of GCSEs to complete. My mother was also gravely ill. So I felt I had no business taking this first offer, especially as I then felt I would find it particularly difficult to cope with all the changes I knew accepting it would bring.

The fact that each year, just after Christmas, there is a pronounced increase in the number seeking divorce supports the fear of some that, were they to give up work, the increased time they would spend in the home might irritate those with whom they share this limited space. Fears of getting under a partner's feet may deter some who are eligible for premature retirement.

Another concern regarding this possibility involves reactions of others who stay at work. Prospective retirees may fear being despised for going off the 'motorway' of full-time employment onto a far less stressful side road. They may dislike the thought of being enviously described as 'jammy' by those less fortunate or brave than themselves, and worry that their motives may be unflatteringly misconstrued. They may also feel uncomfortable about the prospect of being criticised and unsettlingly disparaged by doubters who do not have the courage or chance to leave their own work early. Would-be early leavers may also fear that the very word 'redundant' (even if voluntary rather than compulsory) might lead prospective employers to reject them.

While all these fears and anxieties are, variously and understandably, likely to be experienced by those who contemplate leaving work early, many of them may well prove to be exaggerated, provided that they do not involve any major financial or medical worries. Such misgivings should soon be allayed, once an early retirement that is the result of sound planning and is taken for strong and compelling reasons is actually experienced.

KEY ADVICE

- Ask yourself whether the loss of your status and position as a full-time worker will lower your self-image to a depressing degree.
- Consider how you could make up for the loss of the valued social contacts you made while doing your full-time job.
- Try not to be overly concerned about the shortfall in income your early retirement may occasion. Instead, think of doing other forms of satisfying work, which could, at the very least, make up for this.
- Assess the implications of your contemplated Great Escape on those who may be dear to or dependent on you – especially partners and children still in education.
- Ignore any hostility to your proposed early departure from your workplace.
- Remember that if your redundancy is voluntary, it may not be a deterrent to prospective new employers and that ageism in the workplace should diminish as the proportion of older members of the population increases.
- Take full account of the misgivings and anxieties this chapter deals with, but try to balance and offset these often exaggerated fears against your compelling reasons for leaving early.

3
Planning your early retirement

> To climb steep hills requires slow pace at first
> *Henry VIII*, Act I

OVERVIEW

Prior planning is the key to an early retirement. Above all and as early as possible, you should start a private pension to supplement the paltry State one. Take advice on whether you should make additional voluntary contributions to your occupational superannuation. It might be appropriate to take out one of the new stakeholder pensions, or make yourself feel more secure by taking out critical illness or health insurance. If you do some financial forecasting of likely income and expenditure, you can decide in advance when you could retire early.

The Great Escape featured in the famous war film of this name was possible only as a result of months of meticulous planning. If you are to escape a workplace, especially an irksome, boringly familiar or stultifying and unfulfilling one, you must plan too. Even if your workplace may not have been quite as confining as a prison camp, you must ensure the sides of your 'tunnel' are well shored up and that you are placed in as little danger as possible when finally you break out and so end your long confinement.

In some of its publicity one major British insurer with a large stake in the personal pension business poses these questions:

- When you think of yourself in your later years, what do you see?
- Are you enjoying a fulfilling retirement, travelling to places you've always dreamed of visiting . . . living in the home you

want in the UK or abroad . . . and using your free time to
indulge in your interests and hobbies?

Significantly, these questions are followed by the reassurance that
'there's even a chance you could achieve your goal. You could even
RETIRE EARLY'. But then comes the crucial proviso: *if* you set
the right plans in place *now*. The 'now', of course, is that of readers
who are well below statutory retirement age, for whom the idyllic
outcome of leaving cannot usually be experienced for some years.
It is obvious that the younger the employed start to plan for this
outcome the better. This is all the more so because in the future it is
likely that the already paltry State retirement pension, for which
women as well as men will eventually have to wait until their
sixty-fifth birthday, is likely to decline to levels at which not even
subsistence will be possible.

The reduced value and, for many, the later availability of the State
pension as a means of eventual income supplementation make it all
the more imperative that planning for early retirement be done well
before you actually take it. The crucial reason why at the age of
just 52 I was able to become an early leaver was because ten
years earlier I had acted on my misgiving that my teacher's superannuation arrangements alone would be unlikely to provide me
with an income that would allow me to spend 'life's longest holiday'
in a way I would desire – as opposed to a way I would have to settle
for or make the most of. The action in question involved income
received for self-employed work, unconnected with and quite
distinct from my full-time employment. I used this money to make
payments, some allowably backdated, into a private 'Retirement
Prosperity' pension plan that received very favourable treatment
from the tax man and which allowed retirement at any age between
50 and 75.

As it happens, my personal recourse to this particular type of
advance financial planning was prompted by a key statement I once
read in *What Investment* magazine: that 'pensions remain the most
tax-efficient form of long-term saving and security'. Anyone who
wants to capitalise on the investment edge that payments into both
an occupational and a private pension scheme can give should
start by evaluating their existing occupational superannuation

arrangements. Ask yourself the following 'self examination' questions (many of which originated with Minet Consultancy Services):

1 What level of superannuation contributions are you currently paying?
2 Is there a need for Additional Voluntary (Pension) Contributions?

Whilst the answer to this second question may well be 'yes', such payments may not suit or be feasible or truly advantageous to all who plan early retirement.

3 What is the current level of death-in-service benefit and dependants' pension?

This question, whose answer might perhaps become crucial at some future stage, is seldom asked, no doubt because its implicit morbidity deters many from thinking about it!

4 What is the 'accrual rate', i.e. will the pension be based on – as is quite often the case – one sixtieth of final salary (which may not include commission or bonus payments) being given for every year of service?
5 Will your occupational pension increase to keep up with inflation?
6 Do you have any previous, untransferred or preserved super-annuation benefits involving previous employment and pension schemes quite distinct and unconnected with your present working involvement?

As David Harris has pointed out, any old 'frozen' pension arrangements can be independently reviewed to ascertain whether transfer to another scheme would be advantageous.

Setting in place early the arrangements that will eventually provide the amount of supplementary income needed if the idyll of premature retirement is actually and happily to be realised is not just desirable. It is vital.

It was only after years of careful planning that engineers were able to get rockets to escape the Earth's gravitational field. This image is relevant to early leavers. They have to ensure, while in full-time employment – while they are powered by the most powerful stages of their personal financial 'rockets' – that these have sufficient 'thrust'. By the time of premature retirement, when these stages fall away, they need to be well beyond the pull of 'gravitational' factors and forces that would otherwise seriously constrain their standard of living, leaving them at risk in the perilous atmosphere of their many post-retirement years.

Sadly, too many who dream of early retirement scarcely plan for it at all, or do too little too late. They have little chance of escaping the gravitational pull of their present employment because the cost of funding the lifestyle they desire would far exceed their inflow of funds. Even successful middle-aged professionals may have concentrated on their careers so much that they neglected proper funding of the premature retirement they may sometimes have contemplated.

This fact and the alarming statistic that over 44 per cent of the self-employed have no pension of their own do rather justify the decision of one investment group to publish a brochure promoting its financial planning service that starts with the claim that 'how well your investments meet your need for extra income may depend on how well you plan'. If any employees wish eventually not only to be propelled (like some high-flying astronaut) safely beyond the gravitational pull of financial constraints, but also to achieve this impressive feat as 'early leavers', there is one vital course of action they need to take. As early in working life as possible, they should contact an appropriately regulated financial adviser who specialises in pensions and start planning for their retirement.

In advance of such a consultation, you would be wise to do your homework by studying the performance league tables of companies providing pensions that appear in financial magazines such as *What Investment*. Those considering taking out a personal pension should note that it is more beneficial to pay the necessary contributions via an annual lump sum, rather than monthly, because this lowers the administrative charges involved.

A very effective way of ensuring your occupational pension, when taken on early retirement, will be sufficient is to arrange for it to be supplemented not just by a quite separate private pension, but also by making (preferably many years ahead of your planned retirement date) 'Additional Voluntary Contributions' (AVCs) into your occupational pension fund. Such an arrangement is very tax-efficient and very often takes the form of a separate 'account' within the occupational scheme. As Tony Reardon has explained in *Planning Your Pension*, employers operating such in-house AVC schemes collect employees' additional contributions (along with any contractual contributions that they are expected to pay) by deducting the gross contributions from pay and calculating income tax on the net amount that remains. This is known as a 'net pay arrangement' and means that those involved get immediate tax relief.

An employee with an occupational pension is allowed to contribute up to 15 per cent of earnings into the appropriate fund, subject to the pensions earnings cap of £95,400. Interestingly, since 1987, the Inland Revenue has permitted 'free-standing' AVCs, whereby, if these are available, appropriate and permissible, the employee is given complete freedom of choice as to where the additional contributions are invested. If such choice is on offer, specialist pensions consultants should be contacted before any free-standing AVCs are made. Another caveat regarding pensions contributions is to be extremely wary of anyone encouraging you to switch your 'mainstream' occupational superannuation arrange-ments from an employer's scheme (particularly one run by a public service employer) to one not so run. The disquiet of thousands who were encouraged (very unwisely) to do this resulted in the many complaints recently made against some pensions advisers.

Currently, the pensions industry is seeking to sensitise young workers to the fact that, with the likely dwindling of State benefits by the time they retire (and probably even more drastically during their long retirements), they need to start building up their own pension funds in their twenties, rather than deferring this until middle age. As early as October 2000, one of Britain's oldest pension providers was quick off the mark in stating unequivocally that 'there's a lot at stake if you delay starting a pension . . . the odds are against you'. Moreover, this company was the first to spell out the major value of a stakeholder pension, not just to the senior 'statutory' retiree of the future, but also to the young prospective early leaver. Indeed, this recently-launched new pensions product has been advertised as a facilitator of early leaving, not just of 'proper' retirement, via the blandishment 'the sooner you start, the sooner you could stop working'.

Financial planning for premature retirement should also consider whether any sum(s) or sources of income may come available, either at the point of early retirement or during what may well prove to be its long sequel.

For example, in advance and in anticipation of premature retirement, the sale of an owner-occupied property and the purchase of a cheaper one could create a lump sum that would nicely augment the sums involved in an early leaver's severance package. Such a sum might also come from an inheritance or less sadly, a gift – perhaps from an ageing parent who wishes to avoid any future payment of inheritance tax.

Those considering retirement should try to think ahead, anticipating how circumstances could change after retirement and start planning how to deal with these changes well before they are experienced. Many providers of financial services have usefully addressed the issue of advance planning for retirement by getting the individual concerned to conduct a 'financial audit'. This is a process of self-examination designed to diagnose then deal with any current weaknesses and, more crucially, to plan so as to prevent any future financial ills ever being experienced.

In September 2000, five of this country's leading financial advisers and pensions consultants were asked (by Helen Nugent in her article in *The Times*) to advise a 28-year-old engineer how best to dig an escape tunnel that would enable him, in the year 2027, to retire early at 55. Several of these experts advised the man in question to secure the financial bedrock of his current and past occupational pension arrangements and any private ones, with as much liquid capital (held in a cash ISA or deposit account) as equated to at least three to six months of his salary. The idea was to provide some safeguard if he were to lose his job. Others advised him to take defensive measures against physical illness, such as acquiring (at low cost while still relatively young) life cover with a critical illness policy and taking out a permanent health insurance contract.

For it to be sound, retirement planning needs to answer questions such as the following 'top ten' (for which I am again indebted to Minet Consultancy Services):

1 At what age would you like to retire?
2 What major changes to your finances are likely by the time of your planned early retirement? Are current income commitments and expenditure likely to reduce or to increase? For example, will a mortgage be paid off? (Many advisers think mortgage repayment should be given serious consideration, especially given the recent removal of MIRAS tax relief.)
4 Are you likely to receive any large capital sums, perhaps from an inheritance or maturing life assurance policies? (See the comments earlier in this chapter.)
5 Is it possible that your children will go on to higher education and need financial assistance?
6 Is your tax liability likely to decline or to increase? Are you making full use of tax allowances? Are you making full use of tax-efficient investments such as AVCs (see discussion above) and Individual Savings Accounts (ISAs) that replaced Personal Equity Plans (discussed below).
7 What savings or investment plans do you currently have in place?
8 Do you expect your salary to increase in the time left to you at work before you take premature retirement? (Note that your salary at the termination of your employment on early retirement is often the starting point for determining the amount of pension you initially receive.)
9 How many people will you be providing for on early retirement?
10 Do you plan to move house on retirement?

Whilst it is sensible to approach first the planning of retirement and then the experiencing of it (whether it is taken early or later) in terms of actions to be taken at various ages – which is why guides like *Investing in your Forties* have been published – such age categorisations can be simplified. In fact, the actions involved need to be taken during just *two* fairly protracted stages of life – your younger working years and your later 'retired' ones. If you sub-divide the span of time over which financial planning is likely to be feasible (which starts when most workers are in their mid-twenties and may well continue until their eighties), the mid-point – significantly, the age at which, on average, workers now retire 'early' – is 55:

25 – – – – – – – – – – – – –55– – – – – – – – – – – – –85

Understandably, in their earliest years as workers – perhaps their late teens and certainly their early twenties – most young people are so hedonistically and self-indulgently inclined that they do not consider let alone undertake any financial planning for the future. However, commonly from the age of about 25 onwards, young workers may wish to reduce their debts and would be well advised to take advantage of any occupational superannuation arrangements or chances, via employee share-schemes, to profit from the future prosperity of the employers they work for. If possible, they should take their first step up the wealth-producing ladder that becoming the owner of property represents.

Whether employed or self-employed, as early as possible young workers should take out their own personal pension (a stakeholder one, if appropriate) because supplementing what for them is likely to be an even more paltry State pension will be vital when they retire, especially if they do so early. Ideally during this still early stage in their working lives, young workers should also try (using professional advice) to make some tax-efficient investments they can keep in place for many years. Then the capital growth these 'acorns' are designed to produce can achieve large, tree-like proportions.

Those twenty- and thirty-somethings who marry and have children should make, and protect, sound and flexible mortgage arrangements. If possible or necessary given their future hopes and wishes, they should also start savings plans for their children or schemes to help finance their education. Life assurance should be arranged, ideally along with schemes to deal with any loss of earnings through critical illness. Further wealth-enhancing movements up the property ladder may be made in time. As the years go by, but while they are still relatively young, workers should try to increase or even maximise (perhaps via AVCs) their contributions to occupational pension schemes and to their own separate private ones. Any feasible ways of reducing, or preferably completing, mortgage repayments should be pursued if possible. By now, rather than gearing your investment portfolio mainly to provide capital growth, as was appropriate in earlier working life, this should be realigned (where appropriate and on advice) to provide in roughly equal measure both income supplementation and capital growth.

As feelings of youthfulness recede and early retirement becomes a distinct possibility in the fairly near future, you need to close any gaps in what pension providers call your 'reckonable service': years of past employment in which you have paid into a pension scheme. You should take advantage of any possibility to add to your reckonable service by 'buying in' further years of it. In your later years you are now allowed to contribute to a private pension a larger proportion of your (now hopefully greater) earnings than was the case in your salad days; full advantage of this concession should also be taken. Wealthier workers, many of them self-employed or not in occupational pension schemes, could consider a self-invested private pension, while contributors to stakeholder pensions whose careers have been interrupted should try to make compensatory lump-sum payments into these.

At 55, or not much later, when early retirement may be taken, if this has not been possible previously, an outstanding mortgage could be substantially reduced or cleared. 'Downsizing' to a smaller owner-occupied property or letting out now-unoccupied parts of your current larger one could help make up the earned income lost by giving up your full-time job. So too could any replacement (probably part-time) employment and, possibly to a greater extent, the shrewd investment of your severance lump sum, not only to provide further income but also produce some capital growth.

As it happens, in this second financial planning stage of most people's lives – the period to the right of the mid-point on the age line on p. 27 – the objective of income generation is usually more important than capital growth. You should now anticipate the possibility that your now increased wealth will make you liable to Inheritance Tax, and should plan to eliminate or reduce your liability. Thought should also be given to gifting sums to your children, who by now may be grown-up and employed – perhaps to help them take their first or later steps up the property ladder. Likely substantial future expenditure on items such as a new or replacement car, a son or daughter's wedding, a cruise, or expensive holiday or extended travel, should be anticipated and prepared for by short-term growth-producing investments. Where appropriate, some investments should be made in the name of a non-tax-paying spouse, and sophisticated methods of Capital Gains Tax reduction or elimination such as 'bed and spousing' be resorted to. You should continue to allow specialist and appropriately regulated financial advisers to monitor and meet your investment needs.

As you enter the (hopefully many) 'last laps' of your pre-retirement years, you should find out the precise size of the State pension to which your past National Insurance contributions currently entitle you, and what they will entitle you to if they continue to a particular date. If necessary and appropriate, any 'missing' periods of such reckonable service should be purchased retrospectively.

Thought should also be given to the possibility that you or your partner might need long-term care, and steps taken to offset at least some of the likely heavy costs of this. If you receive on retirement a private-pension 'pot' of £100,000 or more, you may be well advised to wait until you are 75 before you purchase an annuity. Before then you can receive 'income draw down' payments'. Whenever an annuity is purchased, be this in the early or late autumn of their years, prospective annuitants should consider alternatives to standard, single-life arrangements and base their eventual choices, which are irrevocable, on specialist advice.

During these later 'laps' of life, if health permits, full advantage should continue to be taken of age-related concessions on travel, holidays and leisure pursuits. Purchase of attractive, 'perk-producing' shares in companies active in these recreational fields should be considered. Finally, in conjunction with your solicitor, you should check that your dependants will be more than adequately provided for in the event of your demise.

So far, retirement planning has been broadly presented as involving action during two stages of life: your 'working' years and your 'retired' years. But when it comes to deciding what proportion of your investment capital should be placed in income-producing and what proportion in growth-producing investments, look at the pie diagrams opposite. (I am indebted for these to Bates Investment Services and to *Personal Finance* magazine, in whose *Practical Guide to Investing for Income* they first appeared.)

The first diagram, which may suit your earlier years as a worker when you are in the 25–40 age group shows major reliance on share-based investments. These make up 70 per cent of the portfolio, which is designed to produce capital growth with modest income. The middle diagram, which may apply to the circumstances and needs of many workers aged 40–55, shows investments designed to balance capital growth with income generation. There is less reliance than in its predecessor on equity-based investments and a greater reliance on gilts and bonds. Finally, the last diagram shows investments which should suit the needs of those aged 55 or more, who are either at the start of 'life's longest holiday' or have been experiencing it for some time. It shows how, in these last retirement laps of people's lives, generating high income, via professionally recommended investments and strategies, takes priority.

Planning your early, and so probably long, retirement is not merely a matter of getting into place the arrangements that will enable you to become financially secure and properly provided for. Those who feel, understandably enough, that modern life is too dominated by material issues and monetary concerns do not need to be reminded that retirement is for living as well as for receiving money. But anyone contemplating a potentially very long experience of retirement should carefully consider how they will fill their time, as well as their wallets.

Later chapters on 'A New Way of Living', '*La Dolce Vita*' and 'New Ways of Working' suggest how the time made available by leaving work early can be made really fulfilling. However, because

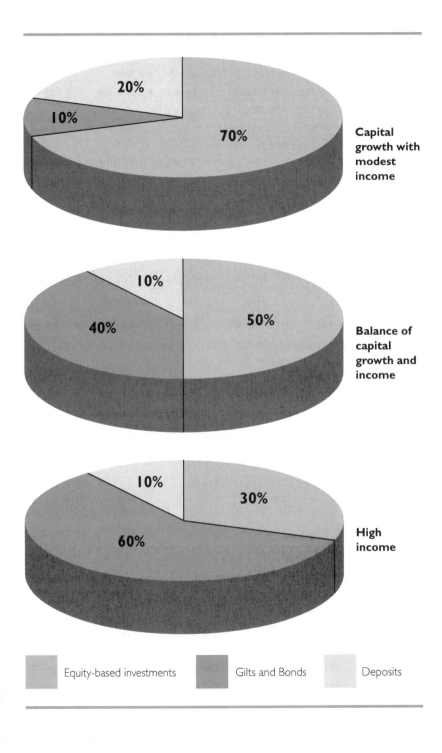

20%

10%

70%

Capital growth with modest income

10%

40%

50%

Balance of capital growth and income

10%

30%

60%

High income

Equity-based investments   Gilts and Bonds   Deposits

every early leaver will find that the loss of full-time employment leaves a gap in their lives, you would do well to think hard before actually leaving work of ways you could bridge this.

In other words, as a prospective early leaver working out your last days in full-time employment, you should also work out how you plan to replace what has extensively and repeatedly occupied so many of your waking hours.

That many who retire need help to find a fulfilling replacement for their old jobs has been recognised by enlightened employers. These employers, well in advance of both statutory and premature departures of members of their staff, organise courses, talks or seminars or present them with retirement planning packs, all addressing the issue of developing interests and taking up activities and hobbies whose pursuit could bring as much if not more satisfaction and fulfilment than their old jobs.

Many monthly publications, such as *Choice, Active Life* and *Yours Magazine,* contain articles and advice on fulfilling post-retirement activities, interests and pursuits, and some even organise residential courses to help their readers find or develop these. Such courses are also offered by some employers, and are sometimes run by adult education centres and specialist agencies.

Unfortunately, however, less than a fifth of those retiring receive any kind of planning advice or counselling, or attend a course to prepare them for leaving work, whether prematurely or otherwise.

KEY ADVICE

- Plan early if you want to retire early.
- Take out a private pension as early in life as possible. Pensions are the most tax-effective form of long-term saving and security.
- Conduct a financial 'health check' on your pension arrangements and consider increasing or supplementing them – perhaps through additional voluntary contributions to your work scheme or a new private pension plan. Make any changes only after receiving 'best advice' on pension planning from

independent specialist advisers. One such is Fraser Smith (tel. 0845 788 9933) who for a fee will review your pension and give advice.

■ Obtain the names of other advisers from the Society of Pensions Consultants (tel. 0207 353 1688).

■ Consider the probable financial positions of those of your dependants who might outlive you and ask yourself how they would be affected by your superannuation entitlements.

■ Try to anticipate and estimate, both for early and later retirement, your income, possible future sources of capital acquisition and your likely financial commitments.

■ Decide whether to take out a life policy with critical illness cover and a permanent health insurance contract, to safeguard you through the years before early retirement during which you dig your 'escape tunnel'.

■ Take advice on what to do about any past frozen (because lapsed) superannuation.

■ Contact: (a) the Pre-retirement Association of Great Britain and Northern Ireland, 9 Chesham Street, Guildford, Surrey GU3 3LS (tel. 01483 301 170) for details of courses on retirement planning and coping with redundancy; (b) The Retirement Trust, 19 Borough High Street, London SE1 9SE (tel. 0207 378 9708) about its (sometimes free) retirement seminars; (c) Age Resource, Astral House, 1268 London Road, London SW16 4ER, which provides information about local opportunities for voluntary work, leisure and ways in which the retired can make their expertise available in new ways.

4

Weighing up future entitlements

It never yet did hurt
To lay down likelihoods and forms of hope.
King Henry IV, Act IV

OVERVIEW

When you weigh up what you may eventually receive from your private and occupational pensions and calculate the final value of maturing insurance policies and other terminating investments, you will have facts you need for your discussions with financial advisers about planning and funding your early retirement.

Your calculations and projections should also make it possible to forecast precisely how much your state pension will be reduced, if you retire early. You can obtain this forecast from the Department of Social Security in Newcastle-Upon-Tyne.

As part of the crucial process of assessing whether early retirement is financially feasible, you should weigh up your financial entitlements by way of state, occupational and private pension payments, together with income from any insurance policies that may mature at known future dates and from any other fixed-term investments such as savings certificates or bonds of various types that you know are certain to augment your capital. As for any legacies you might think are likely to come your way at some point in the future, it is perhaps best, on the principle that there's many a possible slip 'twixt the cup of expectation and the lip of actual receipt, not to regard these as future entitlements!

Early leavers retire several years before they can draw state retirement pension. If you feel that receiving the full amount of this pension when you are 65 will represent a vital or very important part of your income at that point in your life, you should, just prior to premature retirement, ask the Department of Social Security precisely what arrangements you will need to make after retirement to receive your full state pension entitlement.

The decision whether, after retirement, you make the National Insurance payments necessary to produce a full state pension at 65 will hinge on the detailed information in the State Pension Forecast. Prospective early leavers should send for this forecast while deliberating whether or not to become actual ones. You need to fill in Form BR 19 for the forecast to be calculated.

KEY ADVICE

■ Request an exact forecast of what the size of your state pension will be if you were to stop paying National Insurance contributions on early retirement. Obtain Form BR19 from the Department of Social Security, RDFA Unit, Room 37D, Newcastle-Upon-Tyne NE98 1YX.

■ Decide, on the basis of this information, whether to continue paying National Insurance contributions after early retirement.

■ Ask the provider of your occupational pension for an exact statement of what you would receive if this too were accessed early.

■ Ask the provider of your private pension for both a low and a high projected estimate of what you would receive if this were taken early and at other key stages in your later life.

■ Log on to www.dss.gov.uk for information on state retirement forecasts and to see what the latest application forms look like.

5

Financial forecasting

I cannot sum up half my sum of wealth
Romeo and Juliet, Act II

OVERVIEW

The loss of occupational earnings will leave early leavers with a shortfall of income, which they can make good via alternative (probably part-time) work. This apart, giving up your previous work can produce savings, for example on travel and clothing, and these too should be included in budgetary planning for early retirement. You need to review your pre-retirement expenditure and anticipate what you might spend as an early leaver. The object of this is to discover possible savings and budget for the future so that outgoings are not cut too close – leaving a margin for emergencies, inflation and any adverse changes in interest rates. Estimates of pre- and post-retirement income from pensions, alternative work and investments should be included in your budget. This will greatly assist your financial adviser to formulate a strategy enabling you not just to survive 'beyond the wire', but live a fulfilling life there. One way to help achieve this may be to use a severance lump sum to pay off a mortgage early.

Even with skilful investment of severance lump sums or deploying them to reduce or even remove large financial commitments such as mortgage payments, early leavers are likely to find themselves with less to spend than when they were in full-time employment. This will probably be so whether or not they take up replacement paid work.

However, this need not constitute a problem if you anticipated it prior to taking premature retirement, and you realise that not going to work every day can produce considerable savings.

You should try to quantify these savings well in advance of leaving your full-time work, as well as determining other possible savings from which you might benefit when in early retirement.

In the words of a well-known building society, the secret of successful, but not damaging, economising and efficient budgeting, is not to 'cut your outgoings too closely, but to leave a margin that takes account of emergencies, inflation and possible interest rate changes'. In practice, it may be best to compile, using a form of 'double-entry bookkeeping', records and estimates of both your pre- and post-retirement income and expenditure. A budget planning checklist such as the two on page 39 may help you do this. For it to do so, it must cover all your known and anticipated expenditure and also, like a tax return, include full and accurate information (or realistic estimates) of income received when in full-time employment, together with income from your occupational and/or private pension and any investments and payments for paid work after you have 'retired'.

With your forecasts in hand, you have the information which your professional advisers will need if they are to help in the process of securing your financial future. In my case, financial forecasting carried out on the eve of early retirement revealed that using my lump sum to repay my outstanding mortgage debt would greatly reduce my monthly outgoings, as would the removal of the need both to buy formal clothes for work and to bear the cost of travelling 40 miles a day to appear in them. My forecasts – far more than a mere 'back of an envelope' guess – also showed that my decision (based on a precise forecast of my eventual state pension at age 65) not to go on paying National Insurance contributions would also produce a considerable annual saving!

If as an early leaver you wish to allay worries about how to manage in retirement on limited income, note that *Choice* magazine recently described a budgeting system used by one of its readers. You may find it useful, along with the considerations listed by Towry Law and the steps set out by the Retirement Planning Council of Ireland.

Make out a personal budget

Just as the Chancellor has to keep the books and know what is coming in and going out, it can help anyone whose income is limited to work to a system. This is one suggested by *Choice* reader and former accountant Mr J P of Newtown.

First A, work out a weekly income which comes from pensions, interest on savings, dividends, after deducting income tax which you expect to pay.

Second B, list all regular, fairly fixed expenses: if annual divide by 52 to give a weekly amount. The outgoings would include council tax, water rates, gas, electricity, telephone, insurance (house, building, personal, car), road tax, TV licence, club fees (for sport or hobbies), postage.

Now deduct B from A to find what is available for the weekly variable living expenses.

C is for exceptional items (such as a holiday, birthday gifts, clothes), too large to be met by weekly income.

Now you need a housekeeping book, each page to show a month divided into weeks with columns, with an extra column in which you keep a running total carried on from page to page, to show how much you have under or over spent from 6 April, the start of the tax year. You can create something similar on a home computer if you prefer.

Such a system highlights where the money goes and the sooner you start it after retirement, the sooner you learn to live within your income to enjoy the lifestyle you prize.

Source: Choice magazine

Points to consider in calculating your retirement income:

- Weekly living costs
- Leisure and sports activities

- Dining out and entertaining
- Holidays and weekend breaks
- Insurances
- Income tax/Council tax

- Bills and outgoings
- House decoration and maintenance
- Replacement of appliances
- New cars in the future
- Ongoing motoring costs, car servicing and repairs

Source: Towry Law Group

Budgeting – simple steps to follow

Income	Now	After	Expenditure	Now	After
Wage or salary (gross)			Income tax		
Overtime			Pension scheme		
Commission			NI contributions		
Bonus			Subscriptions		
Self-employment			Mortgage repayments/rent		
Investment income			Credit cards		
Dividends			Bank charges		
Rental income			Loan interest/ rentals		
Interest (bank or PO)			Licence (TV/dog)		
Spare time earnings			Insurance/life, home, etc.		
Company house			Medical care		
Company car			Electricity/gas/fuel		
Job perks			Rates (water, etc.)		
Company pension			Food and household items		
Company pension (previous employment)			Pocket money: his/hers		
Disability payment			Reading material/ newspapers		
Unemployment benefit			Travel/holidays		
Pension private			Entertainment and eating out		
Other income not listed			Car (insurance/ fuel/service/tax)		
			Clothing		
			Laundry and dry cleaning		
			Home/garden (upkeep)		
			Presents and gifts		
			Postage and telephone		
			Education		
			Furniture/electrical		
			Charities/church dues		
			Others		
Total			**Total**		

The first step in avoiding money worries in retirement is to start filling out the above checklist, and balance it weekly or monthly. You can then easily identify specific areas where you may be able to make savings.

Source: Retirement Planning Council of Ireland, 27–29 Lower Pembroke Street, Dublin 2. Tel: 01-6613138. Fax: 01-6611368.

KEY ADVICE

- Consider taking on alternative, possibly part-time, work to replace the income you will lose on early retirement.
- Draw up a budget forecast of your likely income and expenditure as an early leaver.
- Try not to cut your outgoings too closely; leave yourself a margin to cover emergencies, inflation and adverse interest rate changes.
- Compile statements of your current projected future expenditure and income, to provide the starting point for discussions with your financial advisers.
- Consider paying off any mortgage debt early so as to reduce your outgoings.

6

Making applications for early retirement

Put on the dauntless spirit of resolution
King John, Act V

OVERVIEW

Applying for early retirement is often a more drawn-out process than you might imagine. It should include a number of considerations, such as possible enhancement of your occupational pension by your employer, bridging any gaps in your past pensionable service, and any chances you have to buy in superannuation for any unworked years. Your trade union representative and solicitor could help you both improve the terms of any offer of early retirement and deal with the uncertainty and tension you may feel before your application is granted.

Whether to apply for or accept an offer of early retirement is a major question. It may well preoccupy those involved for a surprisingly long time.

There are, of course, people who through inescapable management decisions or ill health, have no choice but to become early leavers, but a large number of those who take premature retirement do so out of choice. Generally, this involves their acceptance of terms offered by managements anxious to cut their operating costs by trimming their wages bills.

Many prospective early leavers of large private firms and various forms of public service find the often protracted process of applying for and then receiving or being refused, early retirement is governed by set regulations and conditions. As these perhaps rather fortunate employees approach certain points in their middle life – for example by reaching the ages of 50 or 55 – they, along with colleagues also in this position, may well receive copies of a generally worded blanket invitation to apply for premature retirement.

Sometimes, employers issuing these invitations explain why they are doing so. The reasons they are given often involve 'having to effect reductions in expenditure budgets'. This was so in the particular invitation – to consider making an application for premature retirement with redundancy – that, one day at work, shortly after I had reached the age of 50, I (along with similarly placed 'oldies') happened to find in the internal mail!

Of course, such an invitation has to explain how those who might be eligible to receive it can find out their various entitlements on premature retirement. So the first step for those receiving such invitations is to ask for estimates of these entitlements and to consult with trade union representatives.

Once such estimates have been received, you should check them, again possibly with the help of your union. In practice, the estimates should indicate what would be your exact length of reckonable service to the proposed date of your possible early leaving, any enhancement of this service that may be being offered by way of 'free' gifted additional years that you would not have actually served, and the size of any lump sum payments that make up additional parts of the early retirement 'package' on offer.

When these estimates of reckonable service are sent out, so too may be advice on how – prior to, or on, early retirement – extra periods of service can, if permissible, be 'bought in' to increase your pension and lump sum entitlements as an early leaver. Advice from union officials and financial consultants should be sought on the advisability of taking up this possibility. In your meetings with these advisers, you should discuss, as well as your occupational pension, the wisdom of bridging any gaps in your past reckonable service.

In my own case, buying back for under £50 a whole year's worth of superannuation contributions that, 30 years earlier (during my salad days when money was tight and all talk of pensions seemed irrelevant) I had arranged to have repaid to me, was the best-value pre-premature retirement arrangement I was able to make!

Incidentally, early leavers, and there may be quite a number of them, whose past service has ever involved part-time work should check on the extent to which this work may be counted as 'reckonable', and follow the procedure that may need to be taken to ensure that it is.

Once you are satisfied that the estimates of your entitlements on premature retirement correspond to the length of service you calculate you will have completed by the date this could take effect, the next step is formally to apply for premature retirement. In some cases the needs of employers and recent or planned changes in working practices may mean that applications for early retirement, despite being subject to general rules, are still granted only at the discretion of employers and so will not produce the same outcomes.

This point should not be overlooked, for it is responsible for the tension and uncertainty which can make the often lengthy interval between applying for premature retirement and learning whether you have been granted this so difficult to live through. Very often, by applying for premature retirement, you run the risk of disappointment. However, if as a prospective early leaver you can take some unofficial and informal soundings on your eventual prospects of success, this risk can, at least, be roughly estimated.

In most cases those employers who reserve the right later to refuse applications they originally invited for early retirement, also allow applicants to withdraw these at any stage of processing prior to the formal acceptance in writing of any offer. In my own case, my first application (of two) for premature retirement had reached the stage at which my Chief Executive wrote to inform me he intended to ask his Board to support my application. However, following a meeting of the Board that duly 'rubberstamped' his approval, a development occurred in my family circumstances that caused me to withdraw my application. This, of course, was quite legitimate because the applicable regulations allowed me to change my mind, even at this dramatically late stage. It still preceded the actual point of no return which only the formal signing away of my right to remain in full-time employment could constitute.

As it happened, in the year following these cliff-hanging developments, my family circumstances fortunately changed for the better. Moreover, the fact that my first application had succeeded augured well for my second. This was duly made and its eventual success prompted me to write this book!

Dear John

Premature retirement compensation

With reference to your letter of 21 February 1994, I am writing to confirm that in accordance with the College Scheme your appointment will terminate on 31 August 1994, on the grounds of redundancy and you will be granted Premature Retirement Compensation as from 1 September 1994, as outlined in my letter dated 31 March 1994.

The best 'Dear John' letter of all!

KEY ADVICE

■ Anticipate that any application that follows an offer of early retirement is likely to involve a protracted, complex and highly-regulated process.

■ Discuss any offer with your trade union representative and, if necessary, your solicitor.

■ Enquire about bridging any gaps in your reckonable service and whether you are to receive any 'gifted' years of unworked service as an enhancement.

■ Ask whether any periods of such unworked service can be purchased prior to your early retirement.

■ Determine the extent to which any part-time work can be counted as reckonable service for superannuation purposes.

■ Expect to experience tension and uncertainty while your application is considered, especially if granting it is at the discretion of your employer.

■ Use the cooling-off period that should follow any decision on your application calmly and finally to decide whether you really do want to become an early leaver.

SECTION TWO

Breaking out – taking early retirement

Section Two is all about the brave new world you enter on early retirement. The opening chapter deals with the initial leaving of your colleagues and your workplace. The next chapter describes the new ways of living that leaving early offers you and the one after that celebrates the opportunities for recreation and self-indulgence it presents. The decision whether to relocate or not is then covered in the following chapter, while your possible redeployment into other forms of (probably part-time) work is considered in the penultimate chapter. The final chapter in this section deals with the vital business of looking after and improving your health.

7
Taking your leave

OVERVIEW

When you actually retire early you may well belatedly value certain aspects of your daily grind. Nostalgic recollections of your time at work could feature in your leaving speech, which is just one of the many disentanglements that leaving early involves. However you depart, the manner in which you start your own early retirement is very much a matter of personal choice.

If one were to alter the claim in the concluding words of the song by singer Joni Mitchell that 'you don't know what you've got till it's gone' to 'until it is about to go', then you would be left with a fairly precise expression of the feelings of many as they near the point of their actual early retirement. These feelings may be influenced by some last-minute re-valuing of certain elements of working situations that previously were rather taken for granted or not fully appreciated. Indeed, the last looks that many early leavers take of long-familiar workplaces may well be fond and lingering, coloured by nostalgia and redolent with pleasant memories of happy, momentous, moving, unforgettable, or comic happenings that took place within these locations.

Of course, there are also those whose familiarity with their workplace that they have elected to leave prematurely has made them anxious to quit it as soon as possible. They may react in much less sentimental ways as the time approaches for them to take their leave.

Whatever their feelings during their last days and hours as employees, those who have successfully sought, or been obliged to accept, premature retirement, will find that leaving their workplaces involves a complex process of practical as well as emotional, personal and social disentanglement. This can encompass tasks ranging from trying – often with some difficulty – to hand over the reins to successors, to removing one's riding gear in the form of papers, equipment and personal possessions that were part and parcel of the sustained performance of one's role at work.

There are, of course, many colleagues to whom the early leaver may wish to say goodbye, whether this is done informally and individually or, in a more public and much more organised fashion. As many publicity-shy, self-effacing and other reluctant 'stars' of the television programme *This is Your Life* know only too well, sometimes they are obliged to participate in public acknowledgements of their achievements and enriching contributions to the lives of colleagues. In the case of those departing early from work, these acknowledgements often involve making leaving speeches – a prospect that some early leavers can actually dread, perhaps partly because they fear some may misconstrue their motives or secretly envy them. Whether this is so, or as in my own case, you relish the chance of delivering an oration long fantasised, thought about, periodically revised and then carefully finalised just prior to its delivery, a good deal can be learnt if you analyse the construction of all the leaving speeches you can remember ever having listened to while still at work.

It is perhaps fortunate that a minority of these are likely to have featured vitriolic tirades or caustic, virtually 'two-fingered' expressions of disdain or contempt for colleagues, happenings and practices at the workplace. It is not often that parallels are drawn between these and the horrors of Orwell's *1984* (although I have heard one ex-colleague wax disturbingly eloquent on this particular theme). Sometimes those departing admonish those they leave behind and echoes of the reformist tones of John Wesley or reminders of the missionary zeal of Elmer Gantry may be heard in some farewell speeches. As it happens, I personally prevailed upon one early leaving colleague not to delineate the hell fire awaiting her workmates!

More commonly and more positively, panaceas for occupational ills or malpractices may be proposed, and even more frequently, expressions of gratitude to particular colleagues and acknowledgements of debts to them may be voiced. Other common recourses are to fond memories, to amusing and interesting anecdotes, and to recollections of past incongruities, ironies, absurdities, and bizarre or hilarious happenings. As might be expected, another ingredient common to what is nonetheless always the unique verbal concoction that is an early leaver's valediction is an explanation of where and when time away from work is to be spent.

Occasionally, as an effective alternative to making a live speech, a specially produced video may be shown to those to whom one is bidding farewell. An example I enjoyed immensely purported to be a promotional study of my workplace but in fact focused on particular eyesores. It highlighted, not the most impressive and aesthetically pleasing features, but quite hilariously, the most mundane, nondescript and tawdry ones! The video tour took in a brazier used for leaf burning, glowingly described as a technologically sophisticated central heating system. This had considerable satiric impact but did so in a manner that left no one watching it in any way offended.

Perhaps such leg-pulling, but of the more usual verbal kind, can have a place in the speeches of those who are retiring prematurely. Instead of harshly mirroring the sometimes far from pretty occupational scene, this approach can succeed by throwing a softer, gentler and much more acceptably diffused light on those deficiencies in the working situation that after all, may well have led early leavers to bid goodbye to it at the first acceptable opportunity.

There is as great a difference between those who relish and really enjoy making their valediction and those who abhor it, as there is between very public and extremely private ways some early leavers choose to make their departures. Perhaps the majority of early leavers elect to sever themselves from long-performed working tasks in ways that, while exemplifying neither extreme, tend towards the restrained, unflamboyant and low-key. This is precisely because they are retiring prematurely, rather than in the 'traditional' way after very long stints as employees that have brought them to their 60th, or 65th birthdays. Perhaps because they feel they have received 'parole' or 'compassionate release', early leavers may believe they have less of a right to make or receive a fuss than genuine 'lifers', to whom the gates to freedom only open after they have served their full terms in the imprisoning workplace.

However (as in my own case in taking early retirement at only 52) it is quite possible to leave work early, but have already served a lengthy 'stretch' of employment – sometimes of 30 plus years. In these circumstances it is unlikely that the views of such employees on how to mark and respond to the termination of this large proportion of the human span are likely to differ radically from those of workers whose even greater occupational longevity puts them in line for gold watches.

Understandably then, most early leavers of long-practised occupational roles generally see the severance of these as fairly momentous and thus choose to mark the occasion in some memorable way. Many organise booze ups, meals or excursions, throw parties, entertain colleagues in their homes or invite them to take part in favourite activities. Orgies and orienteering are not often chosen but other ways of spending time enjoyably and socially often are!

In contrast, some other early leavers desire to keep their Great Escape dark and thus do all their tunnelling and breaking out secretly. A virtually invisible way of departing was devised by a good friend of mine – a self-effacing and highly-decorated former member of the SAS – whose silent and, at the time, unperceived premature abandonment of his long-performed caretaking duties perhaps owed much to his past experience of clandestine operations!

KEY ADVICE

■ Appreciate that as you prepare to leave a long-occupied workplace you may become rather sentimental and nostalgic.
■ Expect, even as an early leaver, to engage in a complex process of disentanglement from your employment.
■ Prepare for the probability that you will have to make a leaving speech.

■ Draw some inspiration for this from the leaving speeches you've previously heard.

■ Consider some form of get-together with colleagues to mark your departure.

8

A new way
of living

O, Brave new world
The Tempest, Act I

OVERVIEW

When you retire early you can experience unprecedented degrees of self-determination and self-empowerment. You can enjoy new freedoms and, for once, have time to live and time to spare. You can occupy yourself within a looser schedule and new contexts of activity. You can bask in the sunshine of new endeavour as well as engage in hedonistic self-indulgence. As whimsically or as deliberately as you choose, you can concoct different daily dishes of activity, each made up of very many varied ways of spending time. Like spinning plates on sticks, each of these favoured occupational and recreational activities should be given a periodic twirl.

Retirement is a time when, perhaps at last, you can take full charge of your own life and do only those things that satisfy you without being beholden to anyone else.

These are the words that Harry Gray, the author of *How to Enjoy Your Retirement*, used to describe the new way of living that the experience of retirement, especially if taken early, can represent.

Interestingly, the words 'a new way of living' come from a song sung by the hero and heroine of *West Side Story*, who long for a chance to take charge of their own way of living and to live without being beholden to others who seek to do their self-determination for them.

Early leavers, like the leading lights of *West Side Story* and *Romeo and Juliet*, may still have their youthful vigour but have the edge over those luckless lovers. They are able, on premature retirement, to remove the limitations on their freedom of action that during their full-time employment have prevented the full realisation of their wishes. Early leavers are also lucky in that they find themselves, in more words from *West Side Story*, with 'time to live' and 'time to spare' in which to achieve a degree of wish fulfilment that the hero and heroine of that epic could long for, fondly imagine, but in the end only dream about.

Whatever the particular wishes that early leavers want to fulfil (Chapter One covers some possible ones, such as change of occupation; more extensive pursuit of favoured hobbies, pastimes, interests, and recreations; entrepreneurial, philanthropic or creative activity; travel and taking holidays), any attempt to satisfy these wishes will be made in a context of activity and follow a time scale and a schedule that are likely to be very different from those which applied in the days of full-time employment.

With the acquisition of 'time to live and time to spare' comes the question of how this time is to be apportioned and managed. For some early leavers, the answer to this question may be less clear cut and sometimes less disciplined than was the case when they were in full-time employment. This is especially likely if their employment involved few or no independently performed functions, little intellectual activity or decision-making, and did not require much initiative to be shown or responsibility to be taken.

Those who for long periods in the past have been largely compliant, instruction-obeying, direction-accepting and 'other-directed' workers, who seldom had to do more than carry out occupational tasks, may have been conditioned into a dependence on such a routine. They may therefore be unaware of how lost and paralysed they could feel when the strings that have long controlled their actions as occupational puppets are removed on their early retirement.

Such people might find great difficulty in managing and happily filling the long stretches of free time that early leaving would present to them. For many of them, volunteering for premature retirement could prove ill-advised.

Fortunately, for many others who decide to take premature retirement the inescapable question of how to apportion their time is much easier to answer. This is because they are retiring very much out of a desire to follow courses of self-determination and self-realisation whose charting they have already begun and whose directions are, if only in part, already known and not just dreamt of or eagerly anticipated.

In my own fortunate case, twelve years prior to early retirement, I was granted a sabbatical, or so-called 'year off', in which to study for a master's degree. In that year I gained some revealing personal experience of managing my life and time free of occupational constraints. Indeed, the long piece of writing I had to produce for my master's thesis, not only represented work that was radically different from that I had long performed, but was so enjoyable I vowed that before I made any application for early retirement, I would try to establish myself as an income-receiving part-time writer.

I was freed for a year from my customary occupation, not to be idle but rather to achieve something tangible through work that was absorbing, largely independently performed and very different from my past daily grind. Having coped happily with that experience, I realised that as soon as any chance came my way to take full control of the course of my life, I should not just welcome it, but seize it with relish.

Whatever the new ways of living their lives early leavers adopt – and some may bear little or no resemblance to the ways they have long earnt their living – these are unlikely to prove deeply satisfying if they have everything to do with self-indulgent hedonism and nothing at all to do with work of any kind. Indeed, Harry Gray, after wisely pointing out in *How To Enjoy Your Retirement* that 'the best way to get the most out of retirement is to retire as early as you can', then adds the qualification 'but you don't have to stop working'.

Work, of course, comes in a variety of forms and is performed for many different motives. Interestingly, this is what American careers adviser Richard Nelson Bolles concentrates on in his well-known book *What Color Is Your Parachute?* One particular occupational motive Bolles does not recommend is to want to perform a particular kind of work because it corresponds exactly to what you have long done for your last employer. One of the sights I found most depressing where I last worked full time was that of many early leavers, almost straight after their so-called 'redundancy', allowing themselves (and being rather questionably allowed) to perform their former full-time work on a part-time basis. O, brave new world, that has such timid creatures in it, was my response. Surely the world is so broad and wide that the opportunity – heaven sent by early retirement – to work in new ways that are extremely satisfying should, if at all possible, be seized.

So too should you grasp the chance, somewhat late but still timely, to ensure that the rest of your working life is as fulfilling and rewarding as possible.

In my own case, though I enjoy going to the races, I do not do this every day because I know that too much familiarity with such pleasures would tend to make me contemptuous of them. Perhaps, like television chefs who accept challenges to prepare meals from ingredients that are changed daily, early leavers should create appetising daily dishes of activity concocted from many different and varying ways of spending time.

I have a very vigorous friend of over 50 whose regular lament is that so many of his contemporaries hardly ever emerge from their domestic cocoons to enjoy pleasurable activities outside them. It is beneficial too for the early retired, especially if they are more active and vigorous than those who retire at statutory retirement age, to avoid spending too much of their time at home. The temptation either to do too little or too much that is just domestic may be made harder to resist by the removal of the need to go out to work.

Early leavers should strive to lead fuller, more varied and more vigorous lives than they found possible when they were full-time employees. Perhaps they could regard the large number of occupational and recreational activities they could engage in as so many spinning plates on sticks, each of which needs a periodic 'twirl'.

KEY ADVICE

■ Relish the vast potential for self-determination and self-realisation that early retirement provides.

- Seek to fulfil wishes previously repressed, marginalised or prohibited by your previous employment.
- Consider the possibility that pleasure initially found in an unrelieved round of hedonistic self-indulgence may pall.
- Remember you don't have to stop working in early retirement.
- Re-appraise your skills, strengths and preferences, and think about the qualities that you'd like to bring to new working and recreational opportunities.
- Decide to spend your days in ways that involve major changes and daily variety.
- Avoid spending too much time at home.

9

La dolce vita

No profit grows where is no pleasure ta'en
The Taming of the Shrew, Act I

OVERVIEW

Your *dolce vita* in early retirement will be all the sweeter if you engage in a rich variety of recreational and leisure-time activities that contrast with your new part-time work. If you are over 50, you will be eligible for concessions on travel and active leisure, many of which are advertised in retirement-orientated magazines. These can help you have the time of your life. If you've previously taken the trouble to fund adequately your 'long holiday' and now adopt a more self-focused, hedonistic attitude than when you were at work, you can take full advantage of opportunities for self-indulgence, travel and holidays, as well as rest and relaxation.

As the cliché goes, one can have 'too much of a good thing'. Early leavers who have enjoyed their work may have come to feel this way about it, perhaps well before leaving it behind. Familiarity, even with fulfilling activities, can lead to a kind of contempt or boredom.

This point, of course, is just as applicable to the good things to which, after early retirement, you can resort as pleasurable alternatives to the long-performed daily grind of your former occupation. In my view, the *dolce vita* in premature retirement is sweetest if it features a rich variety of recreational and leisure activities. These can become all the more pleasurable as a complement to similarly varied part-time working involvements.

As an early leaver then, though in Shakespeare's phrase, all the year should not be 'playing holidays', many of its days should be. While those taking premature retirement may not be eligible, on account of their youth, for some concessions on price and availability of recreational opportunities that can only be claimed by 'real' pensioners who are over 65, similar perks – for example, National Express Discount Coachcards – are increasingly being offered to all who are over 50.

If early leavers need reminding of just how varied are these opportunities, they might do well to look at magazines such as *Choice* or *Active Life* (free copies of which have been made available at post offices). The articles and advertisements in them always cover a wide range, and give an idea of the heady mix of pleasurable leisure activities on offer.

For example, some copies of *Choice* I recently selected quite at random contained an article on holidays in Daphne Du Maurier's Cornwall, another (which I had contributed) on a racehorse owners' club dedicated to going racing on weekdays, and a whole series of other pieces and advertisements dealing with a rich variety of leisure time possibilities for rest, relaxation, self-indulgence, travel, holidays and sheer pleasure. Such possibilities, so often curtailed, foreshortened or precluded by the requirements of full-time work, need be so no longer. Wise early leavers can now regularly embrace them, so as to make their new life especially sweet – provided, of course, they have put in place appropriate planning and funding arrangements (described at length in this book).

KEY ADVICE

▓ Engage in as rich a variety of recreations and leisure activities as possible, but consider combining these with part-time work of your choice.

▓ Take advantage of concessions on travel and leisure now increasingly on offer to the over 50s.

▓ Subscribe to magazines and study brochures describing and advertising these concessions and leisure opportunities.

10
Pastures new?

All places that the eye of heaven visits
Are to a wise man ports and happy havens
King Richard II, Act I

OVERVIEW

You can improve your lifestyle by relocating on, or shortly after, early retirement. Any 'downsizing' involved can generate further income and growth-producing investment capital. Relocation undertaken when you're still relatively young should give you plenty of time to put down fresh roots and make new friends in a different area.

Many who consider premature retirement find themselves contemplating such new pastures of experience that it is hardly surprising they also consider living in radically different locations. Further, for some, relocation on or shortly after early retirement can be a way of bringing about not just an improvement in lifestyles but a reduction in monthly outgoings. Selling a property that with the departure of grown-up children for college or workplace has become too large, may be not just sensible but, if followed by the purchase of a cheaper replacement home, can represent a valuable means of releasing further capital for rewarding and retirement-enhancing investment.

Many of the conversations I have had with solitary, widowed pensioners in seafront bus shelters have persuaded me that migration to the coast at statutory retirement age, let alone well after it, can turn out to be an experience eventually, or even quite quickly, regretted.

Admittedly, not every Darby and Joan who migrate to the coast quickly turn into bickering Punch and Judy when at the seaside. But this location, like a 'roses round the door' one in too remotely, rural a spot, can turn into 'Paradise Lost' – especially if, soon after relocating to it and before many new friends and social contacts have been made, the loss of your partner forces you to live there alone.

Not all of the many elderly widows (and less numerous widowers) who live in coastal locations eventually see these as idyllic. Estate agents in such areas regularly receive enquiries from elderly residents leading solitary lives through bereavement. Finding yourself sitting alone gazing at beautiful vistas in an area where you have had insufficient time to put down deep roots can seem far less fulfilling than the prospect of moving back to the community you left on retiring, in an attempt there to pick up the social threads of your former life.

However, it cannot be stressed too much that if you retire and relocate early – perhaps when you are still in your early or mid 50s – there is a good statistical chance that you will thereafter have many years to immerse yourself fully, variously and vigorously in the life of the community you join on retirement. Indeed, if subsequently the loss of your partner obliges you to live there alone, you may have no desire to leave your not so new pastures for your old one.

The question of whether to relocate or not on early retirement obviously involves financial considerations. Property prices and their recent rises and falls in various regions are usefully collected in *House Prices* – a quarterly housing bulletin produced by the Nationwide Building Society. If you are happily settled in your current house in your present local area, you may be attracted by the prospect of cutting the costs of staying where you are by reducing a mortgage or paying it off completely. Paying off a mortgage, so you no longer have to spend such a large slice of your monthly income in early retirement to meet your basic need for shelter, can bring about such a valuable reduction in your financial monthly outgoings that any earlier misgivings about being able to manage on your pension alone might come to seem misplaced.

The Retirement Planning Council of Ireland wisely recommends people considering retiring to live in Ireland to defer the final decision until after a six-month trial stay in rented accommodation. Whether you decide to move house or to stay where you are it is important to consider how the housing arrangements you contemplate for what will probably be a long retirement could allow you to increase the disposable income you receive each month. For example, if you are retiring to new pastures, rather than choosing a small house that can accommodate only yourself (and occasionally your whole family), you might consider something larger. If it is sufficiently spacious, part of it normally not needed could be converted into a self-contained and sound-proofed annex you can let, so producing an income during the holiday season or perhaps throughout the year.

Interestingly, study of Income Tax leaflet IR 87 reveals that if such letting of furnished accommodation yields an income of £4250 a year or less, no tax on this need be paid. Indeed, this concession (note that different and more complex tax treatment is meted out to those who let part of their home unfurnished) persuaded me to consider letting out a self-contained annex in my early-retirement coastal home. This would have augmented my monthly income to a tax-free extent unmatched by many other non-property investments.

Such arrangements could just as easily involve unneeded or regularly unoccupied parts of property in which you decide to go on living after premature retirement. Sometimes, and at no great expense, such property (like that purchased in a new area as a retirement base) may need modification before tenants occupy it, but the cost of the work can be recouped quickly via the regular inflow of subsequent rental income. Moreover, early leavers turned landlords who worry that the presence of lodgers in part of their homes might prove invasive or troublesome can always have prospective tenants vetted by letting agents. By paying a further fee, these agents will also perform the task of drawing up proper agreements and collecting the rent each month or holiday week.

If premature retirement takes you to new pastures where you are seeking a new nest, you need to remember that, whilst this move may not turn out to be the last one you will make in the possibly remaining three-eighths of your life, you should nonetheless see it as such. Plan it in a most circumspect, cautious and unhurried fashion. One way of ensuring this is to take the advice of the Retirement Planning Council of Ireland mentioned earlier: after selling property in your old area you no longer want, you rent for a minimum term of six months. This need not be in the area you decide you will move to. Indeed, family commitments may mean that some who retire early do so at a time that is premature for their children, in that it occurs before an educationally convenient time for them to move has arrived. In such cases, temporary sojourns in rented accommodation in the areas where children need to continue being educated until such a convenient time is reached may benefit not just them, but very possibly their parents as well. First, they are freed from the pressure of having only a short time to find a home that is possibly far away from where they are renting. Second, they gain time to think about as well as search for a suitable base or stage on which to play out the remaining post-retirement scenes of their lives. Moreover, renting temporarily, especially if you have paid off the mortgage on your previous property, can allow you to invest so much of your capital, for once liquid, that the resulting income could leave you quite well off!

There are other potential advantages to relocating than just financial ones. Fred Kemp and Bernard Buttle in *Looking Ahead – A Guide to Retirement*, list the following as their 'top ten':

1 The pleasure of a change.
2 New friends and new contacts.
3 Surroundings of your own free choice.
4 The challenge: can you make a go of it?
5 Exploring the new district.
6 Making a new home for yourselves.
7 Taking life from scratch.
8 Shaking yourself out of old ways and habits.
9 The pleasure of visiting your old home and friends now and again, and having the friends come to see you . . . now and again.
10 Finding new pastimes.

For most relocating early leavers, their financial situation on and for many years following premature retirement, is likely to be an important consideration. They must take great pains to ensure they make no wrong purchases of property – especially if rectifying a mistaken purchase will involve precious capital being deployed in wealth-eroding, rather than wealth-enhancing ways!

One who has been extensively concerned with wise property dealing is the financial guru Jim Slater. He reveals in his *Investment Made Easy* that over the years, he has 'been in the business of buying residential property in a substantial way' and sagely reminds would-be purchasers to remember that 'attractive views from windows and gardens are an obvious plus'. I can only agree, for I believe a house with an aesthetically pleasing and soothing prospect can do much to calm, absorb and charm the prematurely retired during the many moments they have to savour it. In the case of my personal early-retirement base, purchased within a year of leaving full-time lecturing in my early 50s, the splendid and ever changing views of a Cornish harbour it offered – which an estate agent described as offering 'an interesting and ever-changing vista' – was a major selling point for me. However, on first seeing this vista, I remembered what previous personal experience had taught me. Other equally attractive views, such as from the window of remotely situated rural retreats of beautiful countryside, can soon become oppressively familiar, even stultifying, if they are seldom changed for other picturesque scenes and not complemented by interesting activity, leaving you little to do but stare at them!

Slater's point about viewing properties in the winter if possible so you can gauge how dull or bright their interiors seem then, is as sensible as his recommendation of south and south-west facing properties and gardens.

During my own recent extensive, if not quite countrywide, search for a place to retire to, I rejected property after property because they were either too close to a busy road or car park, or because it was impossible to park outside or even near them. I finally decided that at the very least, off-road parking, preferably in a garage on the same land as the property I would live in, was an absolute 'must'! I also find myself agreeing with the highly-experienced Slater that two other features of a property are most desirable: storage space afforded by walk-in cupboards and built-in wardrobes, and (mains) gas cooking and heating.

To these desirable features I would add a piece of advice which, had I received it earlier in my house hunting, would have saved me hours of fruitless travel. It is a good idea, especially in unknown or unfamiliar places, to drive around looking for generally agreeable areas in which to concentrate your search for property, rather than in all ignorance and a totally blind fashion, going straight to the parts of the world that happen to contain properties described and illustrated in estate agents' brochures. Sadly, I must have visited scores of these photogenic 'paper properties', only to find them surrounded by congested, impossibly narrow or potholed thoroughfares, flooded fields, blasting quarries, railway cuttings, derelict farm buildings, and land fenced off because of dangerous subsidence, which made me wish I had never read about them in the first place.

At the risk of being provocative or perhaps upsetting some who live happily in flats, I would go along with Slater's further point that basement flats are 'bad for security, dark and often suffer from damp problems'. I would also argue that, whilst a top-floor flat is often the quietest and most attractive in a block, if it lacks a lift, it is hardly likely to suit the retired and may prove difficult to re-sell. Adequate sound-proofing is also a 'must' for flat dwellers.

The present and future possibilities of noise pollution, from nearby roads, overground and underground railway lines, and aircraft flightpaths should obviously be looked into. So too should activity around the property at night, when undesirably heavy traffic and noisy neighbours, not noticed during the daytime, may become apparent.

Slater also points to the advantages conferred on a property by proximity to shops, a railway station and bus routes. Prematurely retired investors in property should bear very much in mind that in the years after they attain statutory retirement age, they may greatly appreciate living close to such important facilities.

Finally, a word of warning. Several builders have capitalised on the considerable demand for retirement housing by constructing new properties tailored to what they perceive to be the require-ments of their prospective purchasers. Some of these accordingly feature proximity to such attractive leisure facilities as golf clubs and marinas.

Whether or not the individual early leaver's self-perception is that of these more senior 'statutory' leavers, who, understandably are the main buyers of these properties, is not for me to judge. What

I can say is that some of these pleasantly situated purpose-built properties, which may form part of whole complexes for senior citizens or American-style condominiums, can represent excellent value for money and be so intelligently designed as to be very easily managed and maintained. However they can be rather socially restrictive.

The key word 'managed' features in my last warning. There is a downside to getting involved in what can often seem very appealing. This is the chance, in true 'to the manner born' style but at a fraction of the cost, to share a renovated and tastefully refurbished historic house with a number of other tenants or owner-occupiers of its subdivided parts. I once bought the converted tack room and hay loft of a battlemented mansion that was the country seat of a famous politician before his departure from politics. However, my idyllic life there, which enabled me to share its extensive grounds, was sadly marred by dissent within the management company charged with the upkeep of these grounds, a long access road and a tennis court. As a result, I left this 'Paradise Lost' and vowed that never again would I assign responsibility for matters affecting my place of residence to a committee of neighbours.

Some early leavers not only move to new areas after they leave work but also build their own houses there! As it happens, specialist magazines such as *Ideal Home* carry occasional features on this demanding, if very satisfying, form of relocating, with accounts of the various *modi operandi* of some of the 20,000 Britons who each year plan and build their own dream houses. Given they often have considerable energy as well as ready access to large severance lump sums and further capital from houses they sell after they have left their jobs, it is not surprising that a sizeable proportion of this 20,000 is made up of the prematurely retired.

As well as reading specialist magazines and newspapers, prospective house builders can attend the *Daily Telegraph*'s Individual Homes Home Building and Renovating Show which is usually held at the NEC in Birmingham in the Spring. Do-it-yourself house building is perhaps most easily done by those who take premature retirement from relevant practical occupations. Although it can be fraught with frustration, if you have the energy and tenacity to see it through you will often experience great satisfaction. You will end up owning a distinctive and bespoke property that caters exactly for your needs and wishes, and also represents an excellent investment worth far more than you, as an unpaid labourer, have spent constructing it!

As for moving abroad to live after your premature retirement, this is a prospect that episodes of *Eldorado* (a now-defunct television soap opera that failed to entice British viewers away from the more familiar location of *Coronation Street*) did as little to make appealing as a later documentary on the subject. This detailed the often desperate experiences of several early retirers from the British rat race who unwisely moved to the Dordogne before selling their houses in this country.

A radical Eldoradoish immersion in a rather artificial lifestyle far removed from anything experienced back in Blighty or indeed by Spanish locals, or making a living in foreign fields by preparing *gîtes* for paying guests are of course just two possible ways, one rather stereotypical, the other less so, of retiring abroad. There are many other ways of living a fulfilling exile beyond British shores. However, all need a means of funding that can sustain them over the long term, for no-one wants to emulate Somerset Maugham's fictional bank manager, whose lotus-eating idyll on a Mediterranean island turned sour when his annuity ran out.

Those early leavers whose severance packages are sufficiently large to enable them to venture abroad in search of possible 'Dunroamin' retirement properties would be well advised to read Harry Brown's *Retiring Abroad* (published by Norcote House) and to learn the language of the country they settle in.

KEY ADVICE

▪ Decide whether or not to relocate on early retirement.
▪ Remember that if such relocation involves 'downsizing' from your present property, some further investment capital could be generated.
▪ Consider that a new coastal or rural location may not ultimately prove so idyllic if you are left living alone there with

fewer friends and family members nearby you than you had elsewhere in the past.

- Take comfort in the likelihood that early retirement may be the precursor of very many years in which you can put down fresh roots in a new area and establish a large supporting cast of new friends, neighbours and other social contacts.
- Consider reducing your outgoings by paying off a mortgage.
- If you are not downsizing, debate whether to let out any unwanted furnished parts of your home. Look for carefully vetted reference-providing, temporary (or long-term) tenants. They should pay a deposit of six weeks' rent, be given an inventory of fixtures and fittings, pay the rent by standing order, sign a tenancy contract, and be covered by insurance.
- Concentrate your search for a new home in areas you like and avoid wasting time chasing photogenic properties in unsuitable ones.
- Spend six months renting a property in an area or foreign country that is unfamiliar, to assess whether a move to this would suit you.
- Conduct the search for your 'Dunroamin' retirement retreat, palace or haven in a circumspect, cautious and unhurried fashion.
- Consider whether argumentative, noisy or difficult members of management companies or high maintenance charges might sour a sojourn in a leased part of a large shared property.
- Ask yourself if, as an early leaver, you are quite ready for, or attracted by, retirement housing specifically aimed at the elderly.
- Remember that proximity to public services, transport, health and welfare services, and to shops (with convenient parking) may become more important to you after early retirement.
- Assess whether noise pollution, especially from traffic and neighbours or because of poor sound-proofing, could mar life in a particular property.
- Work out whether as an early leaver you might get a 'bespoke' property, tailored exactly to your needs and make substantial savings into the bargain by building it yourself.

- Be particularly circumspect, especially regarding prospects for generating income, about moving abroad.
- As far as possible, choose a property to live in during early (and later) retirement that is not only as luxurious and comfortable as possible, but is also tranquil, beautiful and economic – as well as secure.
- Log on to UpMyStreet (the homebuyer's e-bible) on www.upmystreet.com to gain information about particular areas in which you are interested.

11

New ways of working

He is well paid that is well satisfied
The Merchant of Venice, Act IV

OVERVIEW

As an early leaver, long performance of your past work may inhibit you in redeploying your skills into new forms of work. You could perform some of these at home, go out to new workplaces or start a prudently-financed business. You may gain more stimulation and satisfaction if you resist the temptation to take the easy option of doing your former job on a part-time basis.

By the time many come to take early retirement they have performed particular working tasks so long that they have become not just accustomed to but conditioned by them. They may find it difficult to replace that familiar routine with new ways of working. The shackles or ties that have long constrained former full-time PAYE taxpayers and the self-employed can inhibit them from taking up significantly different forms of work once they are freed from these restrictions. As noted in Chapter One when discussing reasons for early retirement, such inhibitions can be so severe as to amount to a type of paralysis.

Many who have long been on payrolls or paid themselves their salaries fail to realise that the work they do after premature retirement need not be the same as they did before it, or involve leaving the house, or even be paid. Early leavers, especially those whose non-working involvements take them away from home on many occasions, might like to consider becoming home earners. The possibilities here are so numerous that Christine Brady has been able to write a complete guide to money-making ideas from home,

The Home Earner (Corgi). Among many others, these ideas include such 'cottage industries' as these:

addressing and circularising services	jewellery making
antique repair and restoration	knitting by hand or machine
beauty therapy	lampshade making
blind making	music teaching
book and magazine illustrating	party selling
bookbinding	picture framing
book-keeping	private tuition
book writing	repairs and alterations
cake making	sewing
child-minding	sketching and portraiture
clock and watch repair	soft furnishing
computing for profit	soft toy making
counselling	stained glass designing
craft work	stone and pebble crafts
curtain and loose cover making	telephone message taking
dressmaking	toymaking
dried flower arranging	translating
English as a foreign language lessons	typing
fancy dress hire	upholstery
fashion accessories	writing newspaper and magazine
floristry	articles

Many early leavers, of course, have a strong desire to embrace new ways of working that take them away from home. One such was my father-in-law who, at the age of 55, left lecturing to drive his own lorry. Some other possibilities for non-domestic self-employment are minding houses whilst their owners are away, valeting cars, delivering pizzas or other goods, driving minicabs, providing the catering or acting as a guest speaker at functions, and cleaning windows or other parts of houses.

Before getting involved in any form of domestically-based or 'outside' self-employment, early leavers might do well to consider the cautionary comment by Harry Gray in *How To Enjoy Your Retirement*. He starts by recognising that 'retired people who have worked for someone else all their lives often fancy the idea of going into business for themselves in a small way, especially if they retire quite early, say before the age of 55', but he quickly follows this with the caveat that while 'it is certainly good to see retirement as the chance for a fresh start, it is unwise to take on too much, especially as far as risking capital is concerned'.

Such a risk can be considerable, as some early leavers who have been seduced by the blandishments of the many charlatans who offer seemingly lucrative, but actually quite bogus and fraudulent, 'home-working' schemes have found to their cost. Even if you organise your own home-based business, you need to be very cautious, as I know only too well. I recall a college principal for whom I worked early in my career, who on retiring, lost so much of his lump sum in setting up a press specialising in poetry that he took his own life. However, provided, in Gray's words, early leavers go into business 'in a small way with the minimum capital investment and risk' they may well find post-retirement entrepreneurial activity enriches them in more than one respect.

A large number of early leavers, sometimes perhaps too precipitately, take up work that corresponds exactly or closely resembles, what they long did when working full time. Many become consultants in their old field and, as fee chargers, make their extensive experience and expertise available to prospective purchasers. Another paid way of capitalising on such possibly very marketable attributes is to see whether they could be distilled into a course that could be offered at a local further education college. As it happens, I am thinking of doing just that with this book: turning it into a short evening course on early retirement. I have already done this with a sports book, which I turned into a six-week evening course on selecting winning racehorses by computer and pocket calculator!

As Harry Gray also points out, many people possess expertise and knowledge that they might like to pass on via an educational or recreational course. What early leavers turned teachers have to teach need not, of course, involve what they have spent years doing at work: it could concern a favourite hobby or spare-time pursuit. As long as what you plan to pass on as a teacher is something about which you are genuinely passionate and can talk about with real enthusiasm, you will be well placed both to earn good money and receive the reward that comes with genuine job satisfaction. That, above all, should be the outcome of all new ways of working that, hopefully out of choice rather than compunction, you take up as an early leaver.

KEY ADVICE

- Remember that any work you do in early retirement need not be full time nor be the same as your previous job.
- Consider becoming a home earner of some kind but be wary of some postal 'home work' schemes that require you to send money before commencement.
- Take the chance, if appropriate, to start up your own business, but do not fund it with too much of your available capital or launch it without a sound business plan drawn up with professional assistance.
- Consider passing on any expertise you may have by becoming a consultant or part-time teacher.

12

Looking after and improving your health

A light heart lives long
Love's Labour's Lost, Act I

OVERVIEW

You may well be in that majority of those taking early retirement who are in good health and you will be wise to preserve this benefit through even healthier living. Self-referral to a well persons' clinic is advisable, as are free checks on your weight, heart, blood, blood pressure and urine. You could change your diet so you eat more food rich in starch and fibre and with less fat, sugar and salt. You should control your consumption of alcohol and take plenty of exercise – ideally via activities such as rambling or 'working out' that have a social dimension and which will get you out of the house. You could make attempts, perhaps via yoga, to reduce stress and depression – although this should be the last thing you experience in voluntary early retirement!

Fortunately most who take early retirement, through choice or otherwise, do so on grounds that do not involve ill health. However, the fact that some are obliged to retire because of this unwelcome development is a useful reminder to the rest of us to do as much as possible to preclude it. The span of human life has been likened to the mileage attained by a car. Just as a car needs regular checking on its condition, so too should 'well persons' put themselves in for regular check-ups. Many medical practices now organise such clinics (often free) out of a commendable desire to practice truly preventative, rather than merely curative, medicine. Premature retirement is a suitable point in life for self-referral to such a clinic. It is, after all, the starting point for a new, hopefully long, journey into unfamiliar territory. Just as wise prospective travellers assess their fitness to undertake a journey by consulting a doctor, so should those taking early retirement.

At well persons' clinics (and the hospital departments carrying out tests for them) an early leaver can receive free routine checks on weight, height, heart condition, blood, blood pressure, and urine. My own attendance at such a clinic, shortly after my early retirement, was prompted in part by advertising by the British Diabetic Association prominently displayed at my local railway station. Fortunately one of the tests I received as part of the MOT-like screening at my clinic showed this anxiety was unfounded, but another test on my blood alerted me to the fact that my cholesterol level was too high. Dietary changes to many more lipid-lowering foodstuffs were duly recommended and adopted. These both lowered my cholesterol level and returned my body weight fairly rapidly, and most welcomely, to what it used to be in my twenties!

If on early retirement you resolve not just to check on your health but also to do all you can to preserve or improve it, you will find much literature in a doctor's surgery. Some of it will deal with healthy eating, recommending a variety of well-balanced foodstuffs that are both fresh and rich in starch and fibre, rather than sugar, fat or salt. Early retirement, of course, brings with it time for culinary experimentation and more extensive preparation of healthy non-convenience food that the demands of full-time working often preclude.

Health-promoting leaflets in doctors' surgeries also recommend you keep your intake of alcohol within sensible limits (all the more sensible if you have invested some of your money in stocks of vintage claret or champagne). Harry Gray, after advising his readers not to let their consumption of alcohol (or tobacco) increase, suggests they take a serious interest in wine, drinking it carefully and acquiring knowledge so they can tell the difference between a claret and a burgundy! There is, of course, a school of medical thought that claims drinking red wine is good for your health, but that school too would remind you that during early retirement, consumption of whatever you fancy eating and drinking should not be excessive.

Some authorities believe pressure of work could be classed as an industrial injury. What is more, reducing the stress involved in some jobs – such as a stockmarket trader – is often impracticable. It is no coincidence that many in these occupations 'burn out' early in their lives or, via premature retirement, remove themselves from the stressful heat of such 'kitchens' well before they reach statutory retirement age.

This recital of the woes of stress-related work is relevant to early leavers because, in wisely seeking to escape the stress of their full-time work, they should not leave themselves vulnerable to another type of stress – the financial kind experienced by insecure freelancers who have to scratch around desperately for work to replace the income gained in their previous full-time employment.

Rather ironically, early retirement can produce stress if as a result of departing from a workplace two causes of it are experienced together – too light a workload and guilt about relaxation. The second of these may be experienced by early leavers who may become anxious over their new roles because they are uncomfortably aware that, through losing their occupational identities, they are no longer judged by what they have long done and by their possession of particular job titles. In my own case, now being able to style myself an 'author' more than makes up for the loss of my previous job title of 'lecturer'. Other early leavers who can claim no new and acceptable occupational cachet could feel disorientated and demoralised. If they also see themselves as lost in a no-man's land of leisure and worth-eroding indolence, they may feel guilty as well.

Christine Brady, author of *The Home Earner*, has written of the shock of losing 'the cocoon of regular paid employment' and how this can cause some early leavers to suffer depression. Immersion in salutary post-retirement non-work activity such as yoga can be a wise response to such depression. However, as discussed earlier in Chapter 8, early retirement offers 'a new way of living' that can be health-promoting, life-enhancing and indeed life-extending. Early leavers who can break the link between their past occupation and their sense of health and well-being can not just take up this offer but savour it. For them, the last thing they are likely to experience is depression.

KEY ADVICE

- Attend a well-persons' clinic and get as many (often free) checks made on your health as possible.
- Take steps to preserve and improve your health: healthy eating, controlling your intake of alcohol, taking plenty of exercise, and reducing stress through activities such as yoga.
- Improve your self-image by reinventing yourself, for example by taking up a new, ego-enhancing occupation, perhaps performed part time.
- Contact the Sports Council, 16 Upper Woburn Place, London WC1, and ask for its free booklet *50 and All to Play For*
- Get in touch with Research into Ageing, Baird House, 15–17 St Cross Street, London EC1 (Tel. 020 7404 6878) and ask for its booklet *Exercise for Healthy Ageing*.
- For information on health matters log on to these websites:
  www.mynutrition.co.uk
  www.fitnesslink.com
  www.hon.ch/MedHunt
  www.nhsdirect.nhs.uk
  www.mwsearch.com
  www.bbc.co.uk/health

SECTION THREE

Prospering outside – financing early retirement

This section covers the crucial matter of ensuring, well in advance, that when you want to retire early it is financially feasible for you to do so. Here you will learn how to find truly independent and impartial financial advice, how to select 'paper' and other investments to supplement income and produce capital growth, how to construct a balanced investment portfolio, and how to invest on preferential and tax-advantageous terms.

13

Finding a way through the advice jungle

Modest doubt is called the beacon of the wise
Troilus and Cressida, Act II

OVERVIEW

Here you will be shown how to find your way through the jungle of financial advice. Reassuringly, you will learn how to get 'shark-free' advice and how to quiz advisers to reveal whether they are genuinely independent specialists or not. You will also learn a mnemonic-based system that will help you understand exactly what is involved in any recommended investments.

In September 1994 a *World in Action* television documentary criticised the advice given to some of the clients of Britain's then largest retirement portfolio managers, stinging them into an expensive newspaper defence of their reputation. This gives food for thought for all early leavers seeking advice on investments from financial advisers. So should the comment by the editor of *Personal Finance* in the same month, that 'a whole procession of financial services companies have had to own up to a series of malpractices and misdemeanours'.

That different financial products pay differing amounts of commission to those who sell them is not supposed to affect the judgement of independent advisers as to what they recommend but, as financial journalist Paul Lewis once succinctly put it, 'this does happen in some cases'. This is because consultants working for some firms of ostensibly independent financial advisers receive little or no basic salary. They can be sorely tempted not to give 'best' untied advice, as they should, but rather to 'push' not necessarily best-performing products whose purchase from their own organisation or elsewhere will bring them sizeable commissions that the investor alone has to fund. Indeed, these commissions are often sufficiently hefty to compensate the basically-paid adviser for time fruitlessly spent on eventual non-purchasers of products.

No wonder then that not long ago the makers of some television advertisements for National Savings products presented the world of investment as a jungle in which you can fall prey to predators. With similarly worrying creatures in mind, financial advisers Fiona Price and Partners produced their *Shark-Free Guide to Financial Advice.* This booklet and another, *Helping You Through the Financial Maze* (Bates Investment Services) will show you how to select a financial adviser, what information an adviser should ask you for, how to evaluate an adviser's professionalism, and where to complain if things go wrong. When things did so for one of the investors featured by the *World in Action* programme, he felt so disgruntled that he travelled to meetings organised by the firm that badly advised him to give his side of the story in person. But there are other ways.

Asking advisers who purport to be independent questions that will reveal whether they have indeed looked at the whole field of investment in their effort to meet your personal needs as an early retired investor is just the start. You should also ask what commission will be earned for the advice being given, for long-term performance records of the investment involved and comparisons between these and its market rivals. It is also wise to get precise information about the costs of both setting up the investment in the first place, of staying in it and, in case you might want to do so at some future stage, of pulling out of it later.

If you ask an appropriately authorised dealer for such information (as well as for details of the experience, investment philosophy, freedom, regulation, past performance and charges of those who will actually manage a recommended investment) and your questions are met with any reluctance, prevarication or evasion, you should be suitably suspicious. Defer any decision until you have had sufficient time to carry out some independent research. You can find detailed data in *What Investment* and other comprehensive and informative monthly financial magazines readily available from newsagents.

During discussions with financial consultants, perhaps as part of your own scepticism, it is important to ask for some alternative proposals, rather as you might ask a builder for an alternative set of plans. These should be fully costed and show exactly what commissions will be paid. Bear in mind that because of the profitability to them of so doing, many advisers tend to steer their clients towards endowment policies and unit, rather than investment, trusts. They are often keen to recommend that some perfectly satisfactory investments be ditched in favour of others, because of the high commissions the latter pay them and despite the questionable advantage of this to the investor. A related tendency of some not too independent advisers is to dispense with, shorten or over-simplify the enquiry into your financial status and needs. This risks writing a prescription for your future financial health whose effectiveness is questionable because it is not based on your particular case.

Fortunately it is now less likely that another major prime-time television documentary will focus on the aggrieved feelings of sizeable numbers of retired investors. Just three months after these feelings were aired on television, regulations came into force obliging advisers to disclose in precise cash terms how much commission their clients would have to pay them when purchasing financial products.

In an article heralding the new controls, financial journalist Wendy Elkington concentrated on insurance providers. She revealed that on policies involving premiums of £50 a month, the following commissions had typically been paid:

- █ £600 on whole life policies
- █ £500 on 25-year endowment policies
- █ £400 on pension plans
- █ £200 on ten-year endowment policies
- █ £15 on unit trust savings plans.

She also made the telling point that 'selling a product with a £100 a month premium can involve the same amount of work as a product with half that and yet the salesperson can earn twice as much'. The rather lamentable fact is that, before January 1995, a financial adviser could disguise any large dollop of commission received by presenting this to the purchaser of a product not in precise monetary terms but rather as a percentage of the first year's payments or premiums.

The fears of past chargers of high commissions that disclosing the size of these commissions would make the products concerned much less attractive may lead some of them to change their arrangements so that initially a far higher proportion of investors' cash is actually invested in these products and a much smaller one goes to fund commissions. What is also reassuring to the early-retired investor is that, since 1995, providers of financial products have been required not just to give prospective clients the right to change their minds, but also to issue them with a 'features' letter that:

■ includes a 'reason why' statement setting out why the product has been recommended
■ specifies the exact aims of the product
■ spells out the commitment which the customer undertakes and the risk factors involved
■ gives details, where appropriate, of potential surrender values of the product over a stated number of years, or of projected returns based on conservative and less conservative assumptions about the state of the economy while these products are held.

Even before it was announced that from January 1995, the law would require financial advisers to disclose the source and size of their commissions, considerable public disquiet about commissions paid to financial advisers led some consultants to offer fee-based advice. Advice is paid for either on a flat fee basis, with you, as the client, keeping the commission, or the commission is split with the adviser. You would then get a cheque for the agreed amount, which you could keep or reinvest this part of the commission into the original investment. The last-mentioned option is often the best, for it means your investment will start off with more money in it.

Using a fee-charging adviser is often a sound way of saving money because an hour's advice can cost far less than the several hundred pounds many a commission-paid adviser will charge an investor.

Fortunately, genuinely independent advice is offered free, without any fee whatsoever, in the publicity put out by several highly-reputable and widely-respected advisers of both early leavers and the statutory retired. One such concern, the Bradford and Bingley Building Society, most conveniently, has a high-street presence.

Finally, here is a checklist of descriptive acronyms I have devised to help you judge which investments, out of all that are recommended to you by various financial advisers, you should take seriously. You could ask each adviser to comment on the features of their recommendations, and use the acronyms to summarise and assess what they say. This should reveal their knowledge and level of expertise, as well as helping you understand the ins and outs of what they are proposing.

Access to capital invested

EATC	Easy access to capital
PATC	Penalised access to capital
NATCUT	No access to capital until termination

Charges involved

IIARC	Incurs initial and renewal charges
IC	Incurs charges
INC	Incurs no charges

Complexity

CI	Complex investment
NCI	Non-complex investment

Duration of investment

FTI	Fixed-term investment
STI	Short-term investment
MTI	Medium-term investment
LTI	Long-term investment

Exit from investment

CLFPR	Charges levied for premature exit

Expertise needed
SEIO   Suitable experienced investors only
SKR   Specialised knowledge required

Financing
LSN   Lump sum needed
SPI   Savings plan investment

Growth potential
DFCG   Designed for capital growth
PNCG   Produces no capital growth

Income generation
PIAPRTC   Produces income at possible risk to capital
PRI   Produces regular income
PAIO   Produces accrued income only
PFI   Produces fixed income
PVI   Produces variable income
PNI   Produces no income
PMI   Produces monthly income

Inflation proofing
IPVRPI   Inflation-proofed via Retail Price Index

Performance
PDOME   Performance dependent on management expertise
PDOGIFTSEI   Performance dependent on growth in FTSE 100 index

Position and protection of capital
CS   Capital secure
CMBE   Capital may be eroded
NCP   No capital protection
SCP   Some capital protection
VOCIF   Value of capital invested fluctuates

Resale possibilities
VERP   Very easy resale possibilities
FERP   Fairly easy resale possibilities
DRP   Difficult resale possibilities
NRPPTT   No resale possibilities prior to termination
NRP   No resale possibilities

Returns
ROCGAT   Return of capital guaranteed at termination
RIIACG   Returns involve income and capital growth

Risks involved
LRI   Low-risk investment
MRI   Medium-risk investment
HRI   High-risk investment

Tax suitability
PSTHRT   Particularly suited to higher-rate taxpayers
PSTSRT   Particularly suited to standard-rate taxpayers
PSTNT   Particularly suited to non-taxpayers

Temporal suitability (i.e. for the early leaver)
VSFMPRI   Very suitable for many prematurely retired investors
SFLSOELR Suitable for later stages of early leavers' retirement

Type of holding
PBI   Possible 'base' investment
PAI   Possible 'apex' investment

Volatility of investment
VV   Very volatile
FV   Fairly volatile
NVV   Not very volatile
NV   Non-volatile

KEY ADVICE

■ Recognise that some financial advisers and providers of financial products have had to own up to malpractices and mis-selling and some have been fined as a result.

■ Beware the self-interested practices of some advisers who principally seek to land hefty commissions.

■ Send for guides on avoiding sharks and negotiating the financial jungle.

■ For any 'recommended' investment, get precise statements of commissions, as well as setting-up fees and ongoing charges that may be involved.

■ Purchase a product scheme, plan or policy only if it is an investment recommended by a number of advisers working independently of each other. Your own research, homework and reading of financial books and magazines should also endorse these recommendations.

■ Log on to www.unbiased.co.uk and www.find.co.uk to get information on independent advisers.

■ Consider taking advice from independent advisers who charge fees according to the length of your consultation.

■ Read *How to be Your Own Financial Adviser* by Jonquil Lowe, Which? Consumer Guides.

■ Judge whether a recommended investment suits your circumstances as an early retirer by assessing its features using the system of descriptive acronyms given above.

14
Deciding on investments

Prosperity be thy page
Coriolanus, Act I

OVERVIEW

In this chapter you will learn how much 'rainy day' money to keep in rapid-access accounts, and how to decide what proportions of your investment capital to place into growth-producing compared to income-generating investments. You will be alerted to over-hyped investments which may generate income but at the expense of the capital invested, and offered advice on choosing reliable funds that have done well and look likely to continue to do so. You will see how to spread your investments to create a well-balanced, multi-faceted portfolio. There is a 'rapid results' course in successful investing, and specific suggestions on the constituents of a growth portfolio – something ignored by many early leavers. You will also learn the detailed ins and outs of particular investments financial advisers often recommend to both prospective and actual early leavers.

Anyone entering the jungle of financial advice needs to be able to get their bearings for themselves and chart their own course. Otherwise you may come to feel your fate is beyond your personal control and your progress may suffer painful reverses.

To avoid financial pitfalls and secure the foundations for both capital growth and rising annual income, the early retired investor should be prepared to do some homework that involves, both reading and study. The problem, however, is that what is available in books and magazines and even some courses in investment, is seldom tailored to the particular needs of prematurely retired investors. Thus the following 'rapid results' course – made up of advice on specific investment strategies and types of investments – is offered by way of essential preparatory reading.

To begin with, one could hardly better the wise words of advice that National Savings offers, without bias in favour of its own products, to the first-time investor. This takes the form of a series of tips.

1 If you need to get at money quickly to meet short-term requirements and deal with emergencies you should consider an instant-access or intermediate-access account. Most advisers of early leavers suggest between £2500 and £5000 is kept liquid as 'rainy-day' money or a contingency fund. The best rates are detailed on the financial pages of weekend editions of broadsheet newspapers. Some of these involve Internet and telephone banking.

   To meet some known or quite likely future funding requirements – say for a wedding or a replacement car – or to take rapid advantage of first-rate investment opportunities when they arise, you should have some money invested in another deposit account from which withdrawals can be made less rapidly. Such enlightened 'cash management' should be an integral part of any early leaver's investment strategy.

2 If you can afford to tie up your money for a while – say five years or so – you should look at long-term schemes.

3 Ask yourself if you prefer a rate of interest that is fixed and therefore guaranteed not to change over the term of the investment being considered, or one that varies as other rates change. Your choice may be influenced by how you think interest rates are likely to change. Investors who lock themselves into rates that remain uncompetitive compared to variable ones that rise may regret doing so.

4 If you always want to know exactly how much you have saved, you may like the idea of an account that gives you a pass book.

5 If you want to be sure your savings keep their purchasing power, look at inflation-proof, index-linked schemes.

Before you decide on any particular investment, you should be mindful of some further considerations. First, before you do anything as a prematurely retired investor, it is important you establish your aims. Selecting the appropriate tools from the vast array of available financial implements requires you to decide what tasks they need to perform.

In the case of some lucky 'early leavers' who receive hefty lump sums and a fairly substantial pension income, the task for their investment capital is not to provide regular income but instead to grow over a fixed period of time. This growth is likely to be greater the longer the time period. However, John Maynard Keynes's remark that in the long run we are all dead is a sobering reminder to early-retired investors that, while far from geriatric, they are hardly 'spring chickens' either. To make the most of your Great Escape, avoid the temptation to tie up too much spare capital in investments that generate growth rather than income. In general, it is seldom wise for an early leaver to select investments which will produce capital growth only and no income, or by the same token others whose aim is income generation only, with little or no growth in the capital invested to produce this income.

Through taking a pension early, even if it is enhanced by an employer, many early leavers will inevitably find they need to supplement this source of income. Often this can be done by investing the lump sum that so often forms part of a severance package in schemes that pay out each month or quarter. Unfortunately, too many early leavers seek to supplement their income via deposits in banks or building societies alone. Incidentally, the latter are probably safer, as disgruntled investors with the failed bank BCCI recently discovered – though with hindsight they should have been suspicious of this exotic concern and the too-good-to-be-true rates of interest it offered. The problem with placing lump sums in deposit accounts, even with reputable and well-known banks and building societies, is that, while income will accrue via regular payments of interest, the capital sum invested to produce this income will over time stand to be eroded both by inflation and long-term decline in the value of sterling. Admittedly, if your money is in a deposit account the interest earned will help to combat this erosion, but as Roger Anderson and Margaret Dibben have pointed out, 'since the war the long-term tendency has been for any money earned through interest alone to be swallowed up by inflation price rises'. While inflation has hardly been rampant in the recent past, neither have interest rates been as attractive as the double-figure ones offered on deposit accounts in the late 1980s and early 1990s. The message is clear: money left on deposit only produces accrued income and its value will decline over time. So only place in these very safe investments just enough capital to meet foreseen future expenditure and unforeseeable contingencies.

Once you have drawn up a personal financial profile which not only takes account of your monetary needs on retirement but also those likely to arise over its (probably) long duration, then turn to the vital question of deciding what to aim for. Should it be immediate or eventual income supplementation, the short- or long-term appreciation of investment capital, or more sensibly, more than one of these to varying extents?

Remember that some investments are not all they seem, that 'all that glisters is not gold'. While not all blandishments to investors featuring high rates of return are the distress signals of concerns about to go under, quite a few alluring enticements eventually come to be seen by those who succumb to them as over optimistic and rather misleading. This is why some financial advisers urge early leavers to steer clear of investments that promise inordinately high returns.

Because so many of the prematurely retired seek income supplementation, they are often targeted by the makers of such promises. In recent years many of these have featured high-income funds and bonds. It is important that you should be aware that some (generally newly-launched) investments which claim high income do so by using capital to supplement income, thus causing the capital to dwindle over time. It is also important to appreciate that some high-income funds offer, in the words of journalist Jeff Prestridge, 'limited scope for capital growth' and none of the rising income that is normally associated with equity-income, as opposed to high-income, funds. So they should only be considered by those who realise the price paid for this high income. The problem with such new or recently introduced, attractively-packaged but untested financial products promising high returns is that their purchasers, while lured by the hype, often remain unclear about just what they are purchasing.

Remember too that management matters. It is generally better to settle for the security and peace of mind of investing with well-known and well-managed concerns, who offer tried and tested products that have performed well in the past and are likely to do so again over the period you plan to hold them. You should be correspondingly suspicious of investments managed by 'unknowns', for which particularly high performance figures are claimed over unrepresentatively short periods of the recent past. Any investment whose performance may have been a flash in the financial pan is best avoided. You should not be swayed by the flashy, most unlikely to be repeated, quite conceivably freakish 'form' shown for just a short time. Rather, look to what is regularly and consistently demonstrated over both short and long periods in the past. Such Micropal-based financial 'formbooks' as *What Investment* magazine, with extensive tables that precisely quantify the performance of products and funds over 1, 3, 5, 7 and 10-year periods, are much more reliable benchmarks than some over-hyped, short-term statistic given great prominence in advertisements.

The management of an investment should be scrutinised not only for its reputation and past achievements, but also for its continuity. It should also be overseen by the Financial Services Authority, which regulates such investments relevant to the prematurely retired as life assurance policies and insurance-linked products, unit trusts, investment trusts, savings schemes, shares, securities and ISAs. Admittedly, consumer protection concerns such as the television programme *Watchdog* have shown that involvement with a regulatory body is, of itself, no guarantee of high standards of practice or service. However, if faced with a choice between a company such as the mighty Prudential, which is directly regulated by the demanding FSA, and one whose name does not appear on that regulator's central register of authorised concerns, the wise prematurely retired investor would obviously prefer the former.

In general the shrewd investor should also prefer a wide and variable range of investments. In the words of financial architects Carr Sheppards, 'history shows that well-spread investments in real assets (i.e. those whose underlying shares can change in value and allow the original investment to grow) are likely to offer the best protection from the danger to financial independence that inflation always poses'.

If you place all your investment eggs in a single basket that is then buffeted and knocked about in an economic storm, you have only yourself to blame for the ensuing damage. To avoid such vulnerability, you should purchase several different investment products and acquire holdings in various funds, markets and market sectors. Such broad exposure can be achieved via a well balanced, multi-faceted portfolio that is modelled on a pyramid. It has a broad base of large holdings in safe investments, and smaller holdings at its apex, which although less secure are potentially considerably more lucrative.

In such a portfolio the proportions of the whole made up by its constituent elements should vary to reflect the particular circumstances, needs, willingness to tolerate risk, tax status and temperament of the early leaver, for whom it is tailored. These proportions should not be set in concrete but regularly reviewed and, if necessary, altered. The prematurely retired, like all who make investments, have to sit out difficult times. However, on occasion, like anxious hot air balloonists, they may fear that, if they continue to sit tight, they will lose financial 'height', the possibility of which by law has to be admitted by the providers of many financial products in their advertising. Or, alarmingly, they may find they are already doing so. In such circumstances you should consider jettisoning investments that for some time have not produced any gain in height, and perhaps more important, relying more on those that have achieved this desirable outcome. If further injection of capital in products that previously caused your financial balloon to rise are now needed to maintain height, then it may well be wise to make them. After all, cutting your losses and running with what has proved profitable is the principle that such expert investors as Jim Slater recommend.

Fortunately, various flight plans and instruction manuals are available to early leavers to help them gain and retain financial height, rather than lose it. These usefully feature the 'pyramid' approach to financial high flying (see the diagrams opposite).

For example, Hargreaves Lansdown (who offer advice on which proportion of an income or growth-seeking, pyramid-shaped

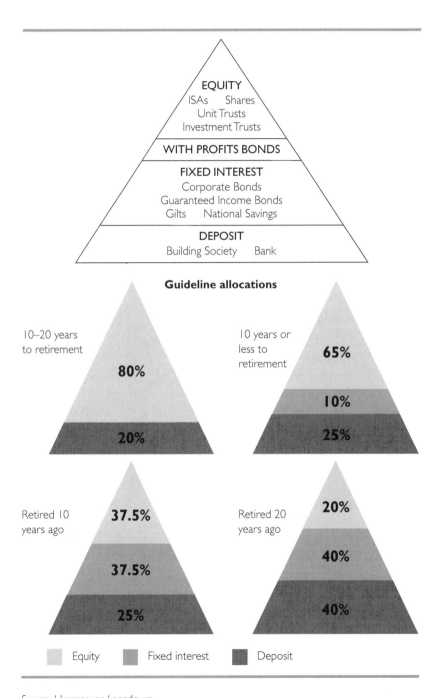

EQUITY
ISAs   Shares
Unit Trusts
Investment Trusts

WITH PROFITS BONDS

FIXED INTEREST
Corporate Bonds
Guaranteed Income Bonds
Gilts   National Savings

DEPOSIT
Building Society   Bank

Guideline allocations

10–20 years
to retirement

80%

20%

10 years or
less to
retirement

65%

10%

25%

Retired 10
years ago

37.5%

37.5%

25%

Retired 20
years ago

20%

40%

40%

■ Equity   ■ Fixed interest   ■ Deposit

Source: Hargreaves Lansdown

investment portfolio should concern UK equities, gilts, bonds, and other investments) provide in their exellent booklet *Investing in Your Fifties* an instructive breakdown of investments that a middle-aged, prematurely retired investor would be wise to consider (see below).

The wide range of involvement percentages on the left of the pyramid reflect inevitable differences in investors' circumstances, needs, aims and aspirations, willingness to tolerate risk, and tax band status. The specific 'base', 'mid-pyramid' and 'apex' investments named in the diagram (and a few others) will be discussed later in this chapter, if they have not been already.

The balanced investment portfolio

Structuring a balanced investment portfolio is actually a very simple matter. Basically, there are only three types of investment which should be considered.

1 Deposit
2 Fixed interest
3 Equity

The following triangle of investment shows this at a glance.

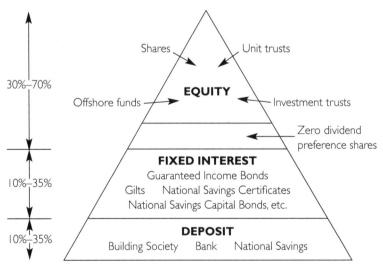

Source: Hargreaves Lansdown

It is important to time your investment so you do not lock into fixed rates which look likely to be bettered in future. Then you will be able to take the tides of investment returns or tax advantage when these are at the flood. A 'temporal trick' of investment that early retired investors can take advantage of is not to put all your stake money down at any one rate or set of terms at just one time. Like professional backers of horses, you should split your total stake and invest proportions of it over a period of time, during which the terms on offer will vary and, quite conceivably, improve. Many people have backed horses in the Grand National at odds they could have bettered if, rather than plunge on their selections at one go, they had drip-fed their cash into the bookmakers' satchels over a period of time! Such phased investment – taking several rates as these vary over time, rather than being locked into one that could come to represent bad value – is worth considering for a further reason: the drip feed can be reduced or even turned off if the investment becomes so anaemic as to make further injections of capital futile!

Many financial products now feature savings plans that involve monthly payments which give the investor the opportunity for phased purchases at varying prices, rather than just one. But timing of investments also needs to take account of the length of time over which they will be held. You need to assess whether this period should be a fruitful one during which yields of income are taken, or a fallow one, in which the absence of any return on capital can be tolerated for the sake of the terminal reaping of a financial crop, whose appealing size and richness results from it having been left alone to grow.

As well as being opportunely placed and appropriately scheduled, investments should take account of a further temporal factor: what the future may bring. This concerns not just changes in rates of interest, inflation and taxation, but also, where appropriate, the fates and fortunes of companies, markets, market sectors, and whole economies.

In this connection, the comments by financial advisors Hargreaves Lansdown in August 1998 are worth heeding. They remark first that 'it can be foolhardy to be too clever with asset allocation', and that 'anyone who could consistently second guess the markets

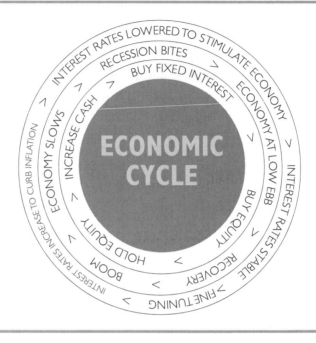

Source: Hargreaves Lansdown

would by now be the richest man in the world'. These qualifications noted, they go on to make the valid general point that 'there is a correlation between the economic cycle and the movements of markets'. This correlation is elaborated in the diagram above.

Hargreaves Lansdown has provided a guide to this diagram, translating its various parts into practical investment strategies to adopt in particular economic circumstances. This reads (in part) as follows:

[A]t the bottom of a recession is the time to reduce deposit and allocate capital firstly to fixed interest. Fixed interest is always best value when interest rates must come down in an endeavour to revive an economy. Obviously an investment with a fixed rate of interest must become more desirable, and thus increase in value, as interest rates decline – investors will buy that fixed rate in the

knowledge that the return will remain fixed even though interest rates may lower in due course. Investors at that stage play a game of nerves. They wait to see whether the lowering of interest rates has started to revive the economy or whether interest rates need to be lowered further.

At some point it becomes the right moment to switch to equity. As economic activity revives, corporate profits improve, business confidence increases and share prices rise (sometimes dramatically). Eventually an economy suffers from full capacity, all those that are employable are employed and interest rates must rise again to curb potential inflationary forces.

At this stage wise investors have already moved to cash, awaiting the bottom of the ensuing period of reduced economic activity (or recession) to move back into fixed interest and then equity.

To the above Peter Hargreaves has added a further qualification:

[N]othing is quite so simple [however,] and there are cleverer people around than the amateur investor and they will be predicting points in the economic cycle and investments will have moved up to two years ahead of the cycle. Indeed, a fully invested to fully liquid philosophy is fraught with danger.

Investing with an eye to the future can also involve trying to spot a wave of investment that looks as if it has the potential to develop, grow, crest, and 'run'. If, like a skilful surfer, you can catch such a promising wave in its infancy, and at what may well be an inconsiderable cost, there is a good chance that it will carry you a long way, giving you an exhilarating and very rewarding experience. Whilst spotting financial ripples that may grow into such waves is perhaps the province of market experts and commentators, the early retired investor who takes the trouble to read financial magazines such as *What Investment* may be able at least to keep up with them.

Understanding the elements and capabilities of each potential investment weapon that early leavers include in their financial armouries needs to go well beyond any mere 'naming of parts' (which, as the well-known poem with that title suggests, can be, of itself a none too enriching process!). An investment should rather be regarded as a home for your capital and, as such, it should be the subject of a full structural survey, sufficiently thorough to reveal both its strengths and weaknesses and to indicate whether the terms on which it is on offer should be accepted or not.

In practice you can evaluate an investment using a mnemonic based on the word 'parts'. Assess, as you might when surveying a house, the extent to which the investment provides:

P Protection
A Access
R Resale potential
T Timeliness (temporal suitability)
S Scope for enlargement (capital growth)

Like the prospective buyer of a bricks and mortar property, the would-be investor should seek out a financial product that is sound, stable and unlikely to be eroded by anything the economic climate might bring. It should offer, as well as accessibility, possibilities for profitable future disposal, suit your time of life, and have potential for enlargement.

When you enter the financial advice jungle, you will meet a very mixed bag of financial consultants, all talking of ladders going up, some sounding more friendly and less predatory than other distinctly snake-like creatures. At first you will hear just a cacophony of confusing sounds. But if you listen intently and for long enough, you will detect some repeated refrains. While the early leaver who wisely takes financial advice from many different sources will seldom hear exactly the same old song in the form of specific product recommendations, you will probably find there is a broad consensus on the general types of investment deemed to offer most to the prematurely retired.

This is because many of these investment products are designed to make up for the shortfall in income that, by its very nature and timing, premature retirement is likely to occasion. Before discussing particular investments frequently recommended to the prematurely retired to make up for this shortfall, here are some points about investing specifically for income, to add to those already made about investments in general.

A warning has already been sounded about the none too golden consequences of some investments that initially seemed to glister. Here, the higher the income promised, forecast, projected or hoped for, the more the security of an investment – the effect on the capital invested of the need to produce these high returns – should be investigated. As David Aaron wisely counsels, investors should 'beware high income products from small banks and finance houses'. Interestingly, a far from small example of a finance house, Invesco, has sounded a similar warning about what they term the 'income trap'. They stress that it is 'important to put your money where it will not only generate an income but where it has an opportunity to grow'. Such double benefits will not always be produced by plans which offer high income but erode the capital ingested to generate this income.

The income-seeking early leaver should of course look for tax-efficient investments, but it is also important to ensure that their tax-free advantages are not eroded by high set-up or ongoing management charges. However, low charges alone should not determine your selection of investments as many quite high charges can often be reduced if you purchase through an intermediary offering discounts. What really matters is the performance of a particular investment and its likely rate of return, after both tax and charges have been levied.

As is apparent from every Chancellor's budget speech, the ways investments are taxed can change. In trying to make sure all your investment eggs are golden, you should aim to put your various income-producing ones into many baskets. But as these baskets are rendered less secure when the winds of change in the economic climate, caused by changes not just in inflation and interest rates but also in tax policy, start to blow, you should periodically check that they are windproof!

As has been said already, it is important for the prematurely retired to work out their actual pre-retirement income and expenditure, and to draw up corresponding figures for their first few retirement years. You should also try to forecast what you will need to finance the lifestyle you desire if, as is quite possible if you leave work in your fifties, your retirement lasts for 30 or 40 years. This last calculation is rather more difficult and you need to prevent it becoming an imprecise back-of-an-envelope business, which because it is too speculative and incomplete, is often unrealistic. An actuary can help here. Important considerations in such financial forecasts are whether your retirement income is fixed, if (and sometimes when) it is index-linked (to help withstand the ravages of inflation), and whether its augmentation is not automatic but at the discretion of pension administrators.

We can now turn to specific investments designed to make up for the shortfall in income that almost inevitably, the prematurely retired will experience. Among the many that different advisers independently recommended to me, a few were advocated over and over again. I soon made it my guiding principle that I would seriously consider such investments, but only actually invest in them if my own research showed that none of their market rivals looked likely to serve my financial needs and aspirations any better.

Many early retired investors who consult financial advisers are told to consider purchasing (possibly in a non-taxpaying investor's name) products that produce growth as well as a further regular inflow of income. Such investments are more likely to be neglected by many of the early retired, for understandable if regrettable reasons. Peter Hargreaves has argued persuasively that one of the biggest mistakes of many early or statutory retired investors is to seek to generate income from every penny of whatever investment capital is available to them. As he sees it, many early and later leavers, all too aware that they are no longer receiving the salaries they enjoyed all their working careers, fail, at least initially, to realise they have reached the wealthiest time of their lives because their outgoings have fallen:

> *The household can move from two cars to one, they sometimes move to a smaller house, their family may well need little or no support and all or most of the material things that were wanted have probably been acquired, or at least are no longer quite so coveted.*

If a reasonable pension is accessible, there is more room than is generally appreciated for a few capital growth-producing products to find a place in their investment portfolio.

Peter Hargreaves has also expressed surprise that the early retired so often place all their assets in income-producing investments, given that they can look forward to the boost in their income that will come when the state retirement pension becomes available to them. This means they are particularly well placed to start a small growth portfolio – perhaps conveniently via an ISA-wrapped unit trust to keep the income free of any tax liabilities. Another consideration is that, once enough income assets are held in ISAs, there is nothing to stop even the retired investor considering some growth now with a view to boosting income in perhaps ten years' time, by transferring the proceeds from a growth investment to an income one that is also held within the tax-avoiding wrapper of an ISA.

As for the size of a growth portfolio, if this is on the small side at £5,000, a good international growth fund might be the first port of call. If, however, £20,000 or more can be invested, then investment for growth could be made in individual economies such as the US or regions such as the Far East or Europe. The early retired investor might also enter specialist sectors such as smaller companies, special situations, technology, financials, energy or healthcare. Nowadays there are funds which invest in specialist sectors on a global basis. The managers choose four or five investment sectors – say healthcare plus energy, plus technology plus financials – and they invest world-wide in companies which dominate these sectors and therefore have pricing power for their products. Hargreaves Lansdown, opportunely, have recently brought out a regular publication, the *Investment Times*, which makes suggestions on potential high-growth investments. A portfolio of such investments can be built up over a period of time, which is often preferable to buying an 'off the peg' growth portfolio at just one point in the economic cycle that may or may not be appropriate or propitious. Investment firms such as Hargreaves Lansdown will tailor a growth portfolio to reflect an investor's risk/reward profile, amount of capital available for investment and time horizons.

Peter Hargreaves has also written *The Gilt Guide* – a survey of Government securities, or 'gilts' as they are popularly known. Early retired investors need to decide whether they want a regular income from these currently rather staid investments or a large capital gain. If the latter, then short-dated gilts, which are usually purchased at a discount, may be appropriate, while the former is best served by long-dated ones. However, as Kleinwort Benson Investment Management Ltd point out, the 'length of time they have to run means that the capital gain to be made when the bond is redeemed is uncertain'. Long- and medium-dated gilts are often index-linked, which makes them worth considering if inflation looks likely to rise. But the low income they initially provide, even though later augmented by RPI increases, can deter prospective purchasers.

Early retired investors looking for an income they can rely on not to fluctuate might consider, if this matches expert advice, a medium-coupon (interest-paying) gilt priced at about £100. Non-taxpayers should buy their gilts through the National Savings Register by filling in an application form obtainable from a post office.

Gilts can also be bought via investment into a specialist gilt unit trust. Stockbrokers (some are readily accessible because they work for subsidiaries of banks) can offer fee-based advice to guide would-be investors in choosing suitable gilts. This at least allows such purchasers to know their fate from the outset. As fixed-interest potential 'mid-pyramid' investments, gilts deserve careful consideration by the early retired, especially when the inflation rate is low, company dividends disappointing and the economy strong.

Perhaps the final word on gilts should be left to Margaret Dibben and Roger Anderson, authors of the excellent booklet *An Introduction to Investment*. Their perceptive view should be of particular interest to the prematurely retired:

> *Gilts are a reliable and consistent provider of income . . . and are tax efficient for many investors. However, care does need to be taken in selecting gilts which are appropriate to the individual investor's circumstances.*

Also frequently recommended to early retired investors are Guaranteed Income Bonds. These investments, unlike similarly low-risk but scarcely competitive National Savings income bonds, are designed to let investors lock into rates initially known and guaranteed for their (generally five-year) duration. As well as a predictable and regular flow of interest on sums invested (of between two and twenty thousand pounds) GIBs, as they are sometimes known, guarantee the return of the capital used initially to purchase them once their (usually five-year) 'life' is over. Generally speaking, basic-rate tax is paid before investors receive their regular returns. However, the fact that tax deductions are not reclaimable means that GIBs are not suitable for non-taxpayers, and higher-rate ones may find they have further tax liabilities on their returns.

The guaranteed returns offered by GIBs make them attractive to some cautious early leavers who want to protect their investment capital. However, the fact that with an investment in GIBs the yield is fixed for some (very hard to predict) further years means this investment can become disadvantageous if, during this period, interest rates generally rise to any significant extent. If this happens holders of GIBs may resent not only being tied to unchangeable and uncompetitively low yields, but also having to incur penalties if they cash in these holdings prematurely. In the words of financial advisers Towry Law, 'if interest rates have reached their nadir' – after which, of course, they rise – 'holders of Guaranteed Income Bonds may be locked into a return which may be overtaken'. Conversely if interest rates fall over the duration of a low-risk GIB holding, the yield will be highly competitive, an advantage to be added to its low-risk benefit.

A recently developed variation of the GIB is the High Income Bond. Early leavers should note that this does not guarantee the return of the capital sum originally invested. Rather, what is returned on termination of this bond is linked to, and dependent on, the performance during its lifetime of the FTSE 100 Index or other stockmarket index. Earlier those with a lump sum to invest on early retirement were warned to be wary of a high-income bond that generates a high percentage of net annual income, providing the FTSE 100 Index rises by a certain percentage during its lifetime. Any prematurely retired would-be investor in a high-income bond is generally well advised to ensure that on termination, it will return

Guaranteed Income Bonds
A brief introduction to a popular investment

When we retired we needed a balanced portfolio of investments. We chose unit trusts and PEPs for the longer term and complemented these with Guaranteed Income Bonds for income and peace of mind and the building society for short term liquidity.

Some questions you should ask yourself before investing in Guaranteed Income Bonds

What is a Guaranteed Income Bond?
A Guaranteed Income Bond (GIB) is a lump sum investment designed to provide a fixed regular income throughout a predetermined term. Furthermore, the original capital investment is guaranteed to be returned at the end of the term. GIBs are normally issued by specialist UK life assurance companies that may be able to take advantage of their preferential tax status.

Are there any age restrictions?
The normal minimum age is 18. There is occasionally a maximum age of 80 or 85.

What are the charges?
The costs of setting up and running the bond are taken into account in the interest rate offered. So the quoted rate is exactly what you get.

For what length of time do GIBs run?
GIBs are designed for a specific term usually one, two, three, four or five years.

What are the main advantages?
- Competitive interest rates.
- No personal liability to CGT or basic rate Income Tax (the insurance fund has its own tax arrangements).*
- They can be advantageous to higher rate taxpayers.
- Interest is not grossed up for Age Allowance calculations.
- Income is guaranteed throughout the term.
- Capital is secure.
- Monthly income can be available.
- No medical evidence is required.
- The paperwork is clear and simple to complete.

Are there any disadvantages?
- If you withdraw your investment before maturity, you may not get back the full amount invested.
- The fixed return may look less attractive if interest rates subsequently rise significantly.

What is the minimum and maximum investment?
It can vary from £1,000 to £10,000 depending on the particular issue. Normally there is no quoted maximum.

What happens in the event of death before the bond matures?
The capital will be returned. The amount of interest repaid will depend on the terms offered by the individual company. Where possible, the investment should be held in joint names.

How often are income payments made?
These are usually payable annually, although some bonds do allow interest to be paid more frequently, such as half-yearly, or monthly.

What if I want growth?
For investors not requiring income it is often possible to allow the interest to roll up and accumulate as a Guaranteed Growth Bond (GGB). Once again the total return would be guaranteed at the outset.

What is the security and protection?
Guaranteed Income and Growth Bonds will appeal to the more cautious investor or to the investor who needs a portion of his portfolio to be invested in a secure environment. It is, therefore, important that the insurance company itself is secure and can meet its guarantees.[†]

---

[*] Levels and bases of, and relief from, taxation are subject to change. The tax reliefs are those currently applying and their value depends on the individual circumstances of the investor.
[†] If the performance of the investment does not match the guarantee given, you will not, for that reason alone, be entitled to compensation under the Investors' Compensation scheme.

Source: Chase de Vere Investments PLC, 2 Queen Square, Bath BA1 2HD, Tel: 01225 469371, Fax: 01225 445744

the capital originally invested. However, there is a case for setting the less-demanding condition, that the FTSE 100 Index does not stand at a level lower than when the bond was purchased. Some confirmation that this condition is acceptable is provided by the past form of this index. Up to the time of writing, it has never fallen in any five-year period since it was introduced in February 1984.

However, as most followers of horse racing know only too well and all advertisers of financial products by law have to tell prospective purchasers, 'past performance is not a guarantee of future growth'! Indeed, if the so far unprecedented were to happen and the index did fall over a high-income bond's five-year lifetime, less capital than was invested would be returned on termination.

However, the level of income received during this period would not be reduced.

In general, in the case of all income plans that involve a particular rate of return over a set period of time, the best time to invest in them is when interest rates are generally high and expected to fall. Broadly speaking, GIBs are a better investment than a building society account if you expect interest rates to fall after purchase. But if you are contemplating GIBs or variants of them, you should in any case reconcile yourself to the possibility that, over the quite lengthy time they are held, the value of the capital sum initially used to purchase them, just like that of a deposit in a bank or building society, may be eroded by inflation.

Distribution bonds are often recommended to early leavers. The aim is to produce what independent financial adviser William Foulkes once described to me as 'a consistent level of flexible income and capital growth on a low-risk basis'. Such is the soundness of the distribution bond concept that two widely-respected investment advisers – Towry Law and the David Aaron Partnership – have made it the subject of special reports. Indeed, in Aaron's 'Guide to Distribution Bonds', specially written for *What Investment* magazine, Kieron Root makes the key point that these financial products were devised to provide a yield on which retired investors could rely so as to augment their pensions.

A distribution bond is made available by an insurance company. It is a generally conservative, low-risk investment in what David Aaron has described as a 'mixture of British Government securities (or gilts), UK and international shares and commercial property'. Kieron Root, in his guide, defines a distribution bond as 'a variation on the standard life assurance investment bond' that 'emphasises regular income payments and is managed in order to maximise them'. The actual income may be taken in the form of a partial withdrawal of capital. Up to 5 per cent of the value of any investment (or higher percentages, but at the risk of adversely affecting future levels of income received) can be taken as income each year free of all tax for up to 20 years. However as Root points out, the idea is that 'over time the fund to which the bond is linked will generate a sufficient return to allow this to happen without reducing the value of the initial investment'.

This last safeguard is important because it places the distribution bond in a very different league from two other financial products. The first comprise those which, if the market conditions on which their projected yields are posited fail to materialise, may have to supply these yields by paying back to investors some of their own invested capital. The second are traditionally 'safe' building society and bank deposits, whose interest yields can, through rising inflation rates, decline over time to a quite alarming and unforeseeable extent.

David Aaron has provided some further important information about distribution bonds. He points out that 'investors who do not require income can have this automatically reinvested without personally suffering tax'. If they so decide, investors in distribution bonds can switch from income-denying to income-providing arrangements and vice versa. The former are useful prior to premature retirement as a means of putting growth-producing financial arrangements into place that can then build up valuable investment capital. They may be used to do this again later if a (preferably planned) stage in retirement is reached when income supplementation becomes unnecessary.

Distribution bonds are not the only investment bonds that are often recommended to the early retired. They share this distinction with what are known as with-profits bonds, which are an even less risky medium- to long-term lump sum investment. Because they involve UK and overseas shares, gilts, convertibles, and commercial property, these bonds are widely spread for safety. As investment vehicles they particularly suit investors such as the early retired who wish to benefit from stock market investments but without the usual risks these can entail.

With-profits bonds are attractive alternatives to building society deposits in that they are designed to produce capital growth on encashment (commonly after five years) and, if desired, a regular, even monthly, inflow of income. This income is made possible via the regular bonuses that, as insurance-linked products, these bonds produce. A terminal bonus may also be paid on encashment. Further, the bonds have the useful tax advantage of allowing up to 5 per cent of the sum originally invested to be withdrawn each year – often in the form of monthly income – without giving rise to any immediate tax liability.

As an investment, a with-profits bond is a flexible as well as tax-efficient repository for a premature retirement lump sum. It also offers the early leaver considerable mileage as both an income and growth-producing vehicle or just the latter, if desired. The David Aaron Partnership recommend with-profits bonds as a first-class and secure medium-term investment, and see them as particularly suited to 'those who want above average returns with peace of mind'. This squares with the requirements of many prematurely retirers, who wisely seek what Aaron has described as 'an attractive middle ground between cash and equity investments over the middle and long term'.

One of the ironies of politics is that Prime Ministers are as likely to be remembered for wealth-producing innovations as for anything else they achieved in office. Thus Harold Macmillan has gone down to posterity for Premium Bonds and in our day Gordon Brown is the man who gave us Individual Savings Accounts (ISAs).

ISAs should receive the close attention of early leavers not just because returns from them are tax-free, but also because of the opportunities they give for potentially lucrative income and capital growth from equities (shares). Because they can accumulate to the generous tune of £14,000 each year if two marriage partners are investing, ISA holders get a chance over just a few years to build up a stake in the markets that is sufficiently substantial to produce sizeable capital growth, or a growing income, or both.

When you consider that a couple utilising their joint annual 'ration' could, after only five years, have built this into a well-chosen, well-spread and highly diversified portfolio of £70,000, you can see that here is an investment opportunity that is potentially of great value to early-retired investors. Recalling the pyramid diagram of possible investments (see p. 94) it is worth noting that its producer, Peter Hargreaves, suggests that investments in 'ISAble' equities such as unit and investment trust funds (and 'un-ISAble' ones such as unpooled shares in companies and stakes in offshore funds) should make up a sizeable proportion, between 30 and 70 per cent, of an investment portfolio.

The accumulation potential and tax-free nature of ISAs also make them attractive repositories for part of the lump sums of the prematurely retired. Just what proportion of these sums goes into ISAs on early retirement (and in subsequent years, on an often advantageous 'drip-feed' basis) will depend on individual investors' circumstances, needs and aspirations. As always, the independent financial advice they receive should take these crucial considerations into account.

Of all currently available financial products, a great deal has been written about ISAs. Although this reflects their potential value to investors, it also means that the result for would-be purchasers, in the words of financial advisers Unitas, can be 'utter confusion'! This is why Unitas attempted to cut a swathe through this confusion by making the following succinct points about the crucial business of choosing rewarding ISAs:

1 Only 2–3% of the population pay Capital Gains Tax (CGT).
2 An average income fund has for most of the recent past outperformed an average growth and general fund.
3 A growth fund which pays very little or no income will only be tax-efficient within an ISA as far as CGT is concerned.
4 If you do not pay income tax, an ISA will be of limited value to you. It will only save you the hassle of having to reclaim the tax.
5 If you are a higher-rate taxpayer who has a large annual CGT liability, you should never fail to use up your full ISA allowance.
6 It is always better to invest in ISAs when the prices are low, instead of waiting for markets to recover.

The second point – about the peerless performance of the average income fund against others in non-foreign sectors of the market – would interest adviser Peter Hargreaves, to judge by the views he expresses in his booklet *Equity Income*. Hargreaves there recalls how his very earliest investment clients' long-standing involvement in equity income funds has delighted them. Over the years these funds 'not only provided income but excellent capital growth and, during lean times in the stock market, they have provided excellent defensive portfolios when stock markets have failed to perform'. He goes on to conclude:

There are many reasons for buying Equity Income. We believe that even growth investors should have some exposure to Equity Income but for anyone who is retired or coming up to retirement we are convinced that a significant portion of their capital should be committed to Equity Income. Indeed I have always said that when I retire, after I have kept the appropriate amount of cash in the building society available for immediate use, I will invest the rest of my assets in Equity Income. I will know full well that I can spend the income on an annual basis, the potential growth in income should ensure that I maintain my standard of living and the capital should look after itself. Indeed I doubt I will even look at the capital values because the only people who are going to be interested in those are my beneficiaries, and whilst I might think better of my beneficiaries, they may be like some beneficiaries, not concerned about how much but how soon!

More recently, Nick Wells, marketing director at ABN Amro has reported (in an article in *The Times* by Kira Nickerson) 'no slow-down' in the demand for equity income funds, despite their recent 'talking down' in some quarters and the recent market emphasis on growth. Wells also noted that 'there are still good income streams available from traditional [equity income] funds'.

Further confirmation of the wisdom of investing in UK equity income trusts is provided in the Unit Trust Users' Handbook *Making Savings Work Harder*. After noting that equity income funds aim to pay a steadily rising income, the authors declare that one of the advantage of such a stake in equities is that 'they usually provide a growing income, as well as increasing capital values which outpace the rate of inflation'.

This useful publication is packed with sound and sensible advice for the first-time investor. It offers the following guidance on drawing up a short-list of possible unit trusts for purchase:

1 Which companies offer the type of trust you need?
2 Can you afford the minimum investment required?
3 If you want to make regular (monthly) savings, is a scheme offered? What is the minimum?

4 If you have some shares which you would like to sell, does the company offer a share exchange scheme?
5 If you are investing for income, check how frequently income is paid.

Early retired investors, especially confident and experienced ones, can involve themselves with a range of other plans, schemes and products designed to enhance their wealth. Some of these are Investment Trusts and offshore funds (which may particularly suit non-taxpayers). Expert advice on these investments should always be taken, and from more than one quarter. More specialised and often more exotic investment vehicles – which may involve more risk than those given most attention in this chapter – are Warrants (to which Hargreaves Lansdown have written an informative guide), Split Capital Trusts (covered by Henderson Touche Remnant), Futures and Options (covered by Irish Life), Commodities (also covered by Hargreaves Lansdown), and 'Zeros' (see the Glossary).

In 1995, the range of available tax-free investments was extended to include three other types of securities – Corporate Bonds, Convertibles and Preference Shares.

Of these, Corporate Bond ISAs are a possibility for those who, on or after early retirement, wish to boost their income. After having wisely made investments in equity-income ISAs as part of their preparation for premature retirement, early leavers could, during their retirement, consider switching some of their investment capital into Corporate Bond ISAs, because the high fixed income these are designed to produce could then prove appealing.

However, the early retired investor should be mindful that Corporate Bonds do not offer the freedom from risk enjoyed by other fixed-interest securities such as gilts, whose very name seems synonymous with gain – even if this may not be exactly spectacular. Indeed, some advisers' misgivings about Corporate Bonds – that their regular and on-going delivery of high levels of income may lead to capital erosion, and that their minimum holding periods of five years may well make their redemption returns subject to losses through inflation – were expressed as soon as they were announced.

Early leavers should also note that a Corporate Bond ISA is only as safe as the company that issues it. This is why (perhaps also with the fate of Barings Bank bondholders in mind) they should consider only holding bonds that are covered by the strong, capacious and protective umbrella of a large unit trust investment spread across many companies. It is comforting to know that the risk that would be created were one (or more) of these companies to get into difficulty has thus been minimised.

Jim Slater in *Investment Made Easy*, puts his readers on the scent of tracker funds, which he sees as a simple way of beating the performance of most unit trusts. Given that many trusts do not achieve performances which match stock market indices such as the FT All Share and FTSE 100, that a tracker fund does match these indices (prior, of course, to the deduction of running costs) emerges as no mean achievement. Moreover, while many fund managers beat returns from building societies, few consistently beat the stock market as a whole because of the difficulties of consistently achieving good returns. So the case for including a tracker fund in an investment portfolio is further strengthened.

Whilst they have never achieved performances to match those of the best performing funds in their sector, many tracker funds have performed in ways that placed them in the top quartile of perform-ances in these sectors. Note, however, that Richard Miles (writing in *The Times* in October 2000) warned that the projected (and any other future) overhaul of the way the FTSE 100 index is constructed might adversely affect the performance of trackers.

Permanent Interest Bearing Shares may well sound attractive to the early leaver but they may involve some risk to the capital invested in them. Were the so-far unprecedented to happen and a building society issuing these shares (in order to raise its permanent share capital) to get into difficulties, so would their holders. This is because, as investments, such shares are not covered by the Building Societies' Compensation Fund. Another drawback with (perhaps the safest) PIBS of several large building societies is that these are sold only in large individual lots of many thousands. However, those of many often smaller (and hitherto) similarly secure smaller societies can be purchased in individual holdings as small as 1000 shares. PIBS are bought through a stockbroker who will charge a commission – which might make a small holding of them less productive.

As Jim Slater has observed, PIBS are a possibility for income seekers who seek a more attractive yield than is offered by standard building society accounts. When interest rates are falling or likely to remain low, PIBS are a valuable weapon in an investment armoury because (technically speaking) they stand at a substantial premium to their nominal value. However, their worth declines if interest rates rise. This market-linked volatility means that involvement in PIBS should be reviewed periodically.

Another disadvantage is that, were the building society issuing them to collapse, PIBS could become a liability because their holders would be the last to be dealt with by the liquidators of the society. However, though such a seemingly rock-steady pillar of the financial establishment as Barings was toppled in 1995, no building society has yet collapsed. This impressive past form is enough to persuade some early retirers to turn to PIBS as a relatively safe, twice-yearly, income-producing investment.

KEY ADVICE

■ Place at least £2,500 in bank or building society deposit accounts as liquid 'rainy-day' money.

■ Appreciate that money so deposited will lose its value over time.

■ Decide whether you are happy with, and suited by, fixed or fluctuating interest rates.

■ Arrange some preferably inflation-proof/index-linked income-producing investments, if suitable and needed.

■ Determine whether your investment priority is capital growth or income production. If the latter, also start a small growth portfolio.

■ Decide whether you require, and to what extent, immediate or eventual income supplementation and/or short- or long-term capital gains.

■ Avoid over-hyped new products managed by unknowns. Prefer tried and tested investments controlled by still high-performing managers.

■ Resort to a diverse armoury of investment weapons that involve you in a wide spread of funds, types of product, markets, and market sectors.

■ Model your investment portfolio on a pyramid with a base of safe investments and an apex of riskier but potentially more lucrative ones.

■ Ensure that the construction of your investment portfolio takes account of your present and future circumstances, needs, willingness to take risks, and tax status. Periodically, but circumspectly, alter its constituents if any improvements appear necessary.

■ Time an investment to take advantage of propitious changes in prices and in the general economic climate (a notoriously difficult undertaking!).

■ Consider 'drip-feeding' capital into an investment over time, rather than making a large one-off purchase on terms that may later prove unfavourable.

■ Invest with an eye to the future, anticipating the trends and developments it may bring.

■ When assessing the suitability of an investment, take account of the protection to your capital it offers, the ease with which it can be cashed in, its suitability to your phase of life when you take early retirement, and its potential for growth.

■ Take plenty of advice from experts but only heed what they say if many of them make specific recommendations that your own research endorses.

■ Research the particular investments – income bonds, growth-producing bonds, gilts, guaranteed income bonds, distribution bonds, with-profits bonds, unit and investment trusts, ISAs, equity income funds, offshore funds and trackers – that, in the past and currently, have been recommended often and by various advisers as possibly suitable to early leavers.

■ Always consult independent, reputable, well-respected and specialist advisers about investments you make prior to as well as during life's longest holiday!

15

Investing and purchasing on favourable terms

I am a man that from my first
have been inclined to thrift
Timon of Athens, Act I

OVERVIEW

In this chapter you will see how to make investments at a cut-price, a discount or on optimal terms via many financial intermediaries, advisers and brokers. You will also learn how purchasing shares in a number of companies that provide pleasure as well as profit can bring you valuable and attractive 'perks'.

As with any service or commodity, if you take sufficient time and trouble or have the necessary knowledge, investments are available at a cut-price, a discount or on optimal terms. A cursory glance at the financial pages of a newspaper or a skim through a financial magazine will draw your attention to advertisements for a whole host of different financial intermediaries.

Some offer so-called 'execution only', advice-free services that involve just the purchase of financial products or services that investors have selected for themselves. In contrast, some brokers make recommendations in regularly-issued reports, bulletins and newsletters, tempting investors by considerable discounts or particularly advantageous terms they can offer on these products.

Early retired investors can, at no cost to themselves, arrange to be placed on the mailing lists of helpful intermediaries such as Hargreaves Lansdown, Graham Bates, Towry Law, Chase de Vere, and David Aaron. Their client updates and other publications cover many attractive investments that are especially relevant to the needs of early leavers.

When you retire early you give up not just habitual employment but also in many cases various perks that employment brings. Once you retire you can enjoy others. Now you have plenty of time and scope to savour them and some can be accessed via certain investments. The Hargreaves Lansdown guide *Attractive Perks for UK Shareholders* has shown that many of the better run, and hence profitable, companies offer preferential arrangements and discounts to shareholders who have sufficiently large 'stakes' in these companies.

In the most recent edition of his booklet, Peter Hargreaves pointed out that one of the best providers of such arrangements has been the giant shipping company P & O. Over the years, many investors have purchased P & O shares in order to benefit from the 'extremely advantageous channel-crossing fares' that then become available to them. Indeed, the very presence of large numbers of private shareholders has 'tended to make the share price attractive'.

As well as previously having provided a list of companies offering perks, Peter Hargreaves also makes the reassuring point that most of the companies on the list are worth investing in anyway, as a means of securing the long-term capital growth that the UK equity market offers. What the early retired investor should consider are investments whose 'value added' elements are as attractive as their potential returns.

P & O are not alone in offering concessions virtually guaranteed to make the early leaver's very long holiday especially pleasurable. Not for nothing was an earlier chapter of this book entitled '*La Dolce Vita*'; sybaritic readers who find those words enticing could consider becoming shareholders in hotel groups that offer discounts on meals, accommodation, holidays, health clubs and hydros.

In their past guide, Hargreaves Lansdown grouped perks in categories, many of which are likely to be of interest to the prematurely retired. Some of these categories are listed below.

- do-it-yourself
- dry cleaning
- fashion

- motors
- property
- restaurants

- financial services and products
- foods
- furnishing
- health
- hotels
- household items
- leisure

- retailers
- stores
- telecommunications
- textiles
- transport
- utilities
- wines and spirits

Hargreaves Lansdown can very conveniently arrange purchases of shares in any one of the 110 or so perk-providing companies that have appeared on its list. Potential investors may be interested to know that this stockbroking firm receives preferential dealing terms on these shares.

KEY ADVICE

- Purchase suitable financial products through the financial intermediary/broker who can offer you the best discount and terms.
- Ask Hargreaves Lansdown (Tel. 0117 900 9000) about attractive perks for shareholders.
- Read *The Perks Book*, published by Butterfields.
- To search quickly for the best deals in home travel and motor insurance, log on to www.screentrade.co.uk

16

Investing on tax-advantageous terms

His burdenous tax notwithstanding
King Richard II, Act I

OVERVIEW

Here you will learn how to avoid or reduce the tax liabilities that investments can incur by investing in a non-tax paying partner's name or by choosing such tax-exempt products as ISAs. You will also learn how to eliminate or reduce Capital Gains Tax, and the tax advantages of making occupational and private pension payments.

So many financial advisers have said that 'the tax tail should not wag the investment dog' that it has become something of a cliché. But the fact remains that the tax implications of the investments early leavers are considering are of vital concern to them.

Tax-efficient savings and how to achieve them are the subject of a special *What Investment* magazine supplement. The vital point is quickly made there: 'tax efficient products can substantially increase your returns'. One way of reducing the income tax paid after early retirement is to ensure that if you have a partner who does not earn enough to exceed the annual income tax allowance, investments should be made in their name. This partner should register with the Inland Revenue to receive interest on bank and building society deposits gross (i.e. without tax being deducted). They should also consider investments such as certain offshore accounts and funds and some National Savings products such as Income bonds that automatically pay interest gross.

As for income tax paying early leavers, their tax-reduction strategies could involve products that, while not giving a tax deduction on the amount invested, can provide tax freedom on the income and/or capital gains they yield. Examples of such products are ISAs, Friendly Society bonds (into which, rather restrictively, no more than £25 per month or £270 per annum can be invested) and National Savings Certificates, whether index-linked or not. However, the currently paltry rates of interest on the last of these mean they should perhaps be avoided at present. You can keep a watching brief by logging on to www.nationalsavings.co.uk.

The capital gains made on some investments such as UK gilts are exempt from Capital Gains Tax (CGT).

This particular tax is currently paid only by about 100,000 people a year out of the 26 million who pay income tax. Whereas the latter tax is paid on income received from investments, CGT is paid on the growth in the value of an investment between its purchase and its disposal. Thus if shares are owned, income tax is paid on the dividends received and capital gains tax on the rise in the prices of these shares while they have been owned.

A recent issue of *What Investment* magazine noted that 'novice investors are unlikely to encounter CGT because each person can make £7500 worth of capital gains each year before having to pay any tax, which is levied at the taxpayer's highest rate of tax'. In the view of *What Investment*, one way of looking at this liability to pay CGT is that 'if your investment strategies are successful enough to yield more than £7500 a year in growth not income, once you have deducted expenses and the effects of inflation, then you have cause for celebration' – as opposed to dismay!

Jim Slater has explained why this is so. Tax has to be paid on annual capital gains in excess of £7500, but if one spouse made no such gains in a tax year while the other had made investments 'pregnant with gains', these investments could be transferred from that spouse to the other to minimise the tax bill, which would otherwise amount to £3000 (i.e. 40 per cent of £7500).

As is also pointed out in *What Investment* magazine's tax-free savings guide, another tax-efficient strategy for an early leaver to consider (if appropriate) is not just to continue but to maximise contributions to a private pension plan that, later in retirement, will augment the occupational pension paid from premature retirement onwards. Such a private pension will itself be augmented when, on statutory retirement at 65, a (possibly reduced) state pension is also received. Most advantageously, contributions to pension plans are tax deductible, and the investment involved grows tax-free. Moreover, exemption from tax deductions is also an advantage of the lump-sum private pension payment, which, most usefully, can be taken at any age after the age of 55.

Pension plans are tax-deductible because at the tax payer's higher marginal rate (of up to 40 per cent) contributions made into them are given relief. The more tax you pay, the more the government adds each time you contribute to your non-state pension. For instance, to make a £1000 investment, someone paying tax at the highest rate need only pay £780, for the extra £220 is paid by the government. What is more, a further £180 can be reclaimed!

Given the generous way pension payments are treated for tax purposes, it is sensible to place as much as you can afford into this particular investment in your future.

If you are an early leaver in your fifties, you can make a single pension contribution and take the benefits immediately, even if you do not actually then retire! With tax relief of up to 40 per cent and the ability to take an immediate tax-free lump sum of 25 per cent of the fund, a mere £3500 becomes the actual cost you pay for a premium of £10,000!

Finally, note that some National Savings products are tax free, and cash deposits are tax efficient if held through an ISA, as are gilts, ordinary shares, unit trusts, investment trusts, OEICs and corporate bonds. With-profit bonds and distribution bonds are also tax-efficient, save for a non-taxpayer, while Zeros are tax advantageous because your annual CGT allowance allows you in effect to take an income (see the Glossary).

KEY ADVICE

- Make investments, where appropriate, in a non-tax paying partner's name, so these become tax-exempt or tax-efficient.
- Get such a partner to register with the Inland Revenue to receive gross (i.e. without tax being deducted) interest on bank and building society deposits and to consider investing, if

recommended and appropriate, in offshore accounts and funds.

- Invest, if you are a tax payer, not just in ISAs and Friendly Society bonds but also in investment trusts that offer tax-favoured income and capital gains.
- Maximise, where appropriate, and for as long as possible, contributions to personal pensions because these receive very generous treatment from the tax man.
- Learn more about taking advantage of tax regulations by logging on to www.inlandrevenue.org.uk and www.taxshelterreport.co.uk.

17

Alternative investments

Dost thou love pictures?
The Taming of the Shrew, Act I

OVERVIEW

Here you will learn about investing in 'tangibles' – non-paper objects such as claret and champagne, classic cars, and collectibles such as watercolour paintings.

As alternatives to 'paper' investments (which, as the holders of some Barings bonds found in 1995, can prove to be worth little more than the paper they were written on) some early-retired investors looking for fairly long-term growth could consider something tangible. Tangibles are investments that you can both enjoy owning and looking at for a while and then at some future point either sell at a profit or leave to your beneficiaries as a valuable asset.

Nowadays, investors in tangibles need not join the 'land and gold and property for capital growth' school of investment, deservedly recommended in previous centuries and indeed past decades. In this new century, other tangibles, many of them aesthetically more pleasing as well as having greater potential for capital appreciation, have attracted the 'smart' money.

The ability of some investments to generate appreciable capital growth was discussed in Chapter 14. Early leavers might wisely consider certain tangibles as possible investments that can not only augment their wealth over time, but also provide considerable pleasure and enjoyment while that happens. Many people could well regard having English watercolour paintings displayed on the walls of their sitting room as preferable to purchasing a paper investment that sits in the vaults of their bank.

Investors seeking to acquire tangibles that can bring long-term capital appreciation and also the pleasure and pride of ownership would do well to acquire a copy of Robin Duthy's book *The Successful Investor*. This is a fascinating and carefully researched survey of forty or so markets in intrinsically valuable entities or sought-after and extensively collected artefacts. When it was first published in 1986, Duthy's book broke new ground with its summary performance table comparing the growth each year over the ten years following an initial investment of £1000 in various objects (see the list below).

- American coins
- Vintage claret
- American Impressionists
- Vintage port
- Eighteenth-century English portraits
- Vintage champagne
- Georgian furniture
- English watercolours
- English sporting painting
- American painting 1910–40
- Meissen porcelain
- French Impressionist painting
- Nineteenth-century American painting
- Chinese porcelain
- Twentieth-century English painting
- Old Master prints
- Regency silver
- German Expressionist prints
- Seventeenth-century Dutch and Flemish painting
- Victorian furniture
- German Expressionists
- Victorian painting
- The New York School of painters
- Painters at the School of Paris
- American coins (excluding MS 65 coins)
- Modern-master prints
- The Surrealists

- Eighteenth- and nineteenth-century silver
- Eighteenth-century English silver
- Chelsea porcelain
- American stamps
- Victorian silver
- The Barbizon School of Artists
- Stamps of Great Britain
- Gold
- English coins
- Ancient Greek and Roman coins
- Diamonds

Duthy's decade-long research revealed that the last item on his list – diamonds – gained less value over this long and fairly representative period than any other tangible. This suggests that as far as financial considerations are concerned, diamonds are unlikely to prove the best friends of a female who retires early enough still to call herself a girl and then either invests in them or receives them from a prematurely retired male who has capital gains rather than any other personal benefits in mind!

Early retirers who have watched their savings dwindle might be interested to know that in a recent decade, investments in many of the tangibles Duthy researched increased in value faster than many stockmarkets, as judged by indices giving evaluative snapshots of their performances. However, Duthy also shows that only one investment in a readily obtainable tangible increased steadily in value every year over the period his book covers, ending up worth almost five times what it was originally worth at the start. This was English watercolours – notably those by the artists listed below.

- Helen Allingham
- William Birkett Foster
- Albert Goodwin
- Thomas Bush Hardy
- Augustus Osborne Lamplough
- David Roberts
- Peter de Wint
- Hercules Brabazon Brabazon

- George Chinnery
- John Sell Cotman
- Charles Dixon
- Thomas Girtin
- George Goodwin Kilburne
- Water Langley
- Edward Lear
- George Edward Lodge
- Samuel Prout
- Thomas Miles Richardson
- Thomas Rowlandson
- John Ruskin
- Paul Sandby
- Archibald Thorburn
- Joseph Mallord William Turner
- John Varley
- William Lionel Wyllie

Of course, as with any investment, past performance is no guarantee of future growth, but that of English watercolours over a long period of the recent past is reassuring. Besides, that a group of paintings should emerge as the top consistent performer over this period should come as no surprise to viewers of the popular television programme *Antiques Roadshow*, for they regularly see the most pleasant surprises at valuations being enjoyed by people who bring along works of art.

You should seek specialist advice, such as that dispensed on the above programme, before you invest in any tangible. Buying tangibles such as English watercolours that fall in the category of arts and crafts, is a risky business if you try to go it alone, without expertise, skill, knowledge, and street wisdom, which together with the priceless art of 'divination', take years to acquire.

As for returns on tangibles, remember they provide no income but may well present their purchasers with start-up costs, such as a dealer's mark up, buyer's premium and VAT, and running costs to do with security, insurance, upkeep, protection and maintenance. You should also realise that some tangibles can gain or decline in value quite substantially, and that such changes come about through unpredictable shifts in tastes and fashion, or what Duthy calls 'the market's view of their aesthetic, historic, functional or some other value'. Another drawback is that tangibles are less liquid than shares or gilts which, if necessary, can be turned into cash at short notice. The rapid resale of some non-paper investments, by contrast, may be difficult to arrange.

Generally, the appeal and the value of many tangibles tend to increase when inflation reduces the value of paper investments. Their owners receive fairly generous tax treatment, depending on whether the gains come from separate disposal of individual tangibles each worth a reasonable rather than a large amount as opposed to selling a collection of many objects as a single lot for a much greater sum. This generous tax treatment makes investment in many separate and reasonably priced tangibles attractive to early leavers seeking a way of enhancing their wealth in the medium to long term that involves neither pieces of paper nor expensive one-off purchases. However, generally speaking individual acquisitions, whether they can be built up into collections or are not combinable in any way, can give considerable pleasure over many years of retirement, with the added reassurance that they are gaining in value during this time.

Recent sluggishness in the market for land and less advantageous tax treatment of using land for forestry present arguments, at the present time at least, for looking beyond these tangibles, which historically were much favoured. Similarly, the vagaries of the British climate and fierce competition from rival wine producers in more equable ones would seem to make investment in vineyards rather too speculative an undertaking for the early retired. However, when it comes to investment in wines the picture is very different.

The investment performance table Duthy included in his book shows that, of all the tangibles he tracked, vintage claret was the best-performing, most-readily accessible investment of all. In his top ten financially best-performing tangibles, Duthy placed vintage port in fourth position, and vintage champagne seventh. This suggests that acquiring stocks of carefully selected wines is something growth-seeking early retired investors could well consider – provided they have the discipline and self-denial not to drink away their investment! Such stocks on past evidence at least, seem to be less volatile, though ironically rather less liquid, than their counterparts in financial markets.

Since 1986 when Duthy's book made its appearance another tangible he tracks, classic cars, have shown declining growth figures. However, early-retired motorists who find their average annual mileage is now considerably less than when they were in full employment, might find it advantageous to try to find a current classic or spot a future one. If they are successful, not only might their investment beat the market by increasing greatly in value in years to come, but in the meantime offers them an enjoyably luxurious style of motoring befitting their leisured status and income level.

This may not prove such a tall order as it sounds, if you look at specialist magazines and heed their advice. You may end up acquiring a machine to swan around in whose seemingly high mileage – which, in fact is quite inconsequential given the car's build quality – means that it can be purchased quite economically. An example of such a possibility – in my case for motoring around the often narrow thoroughfares of my deliberately chosen early retirement county of Cornwall, in a manner as flamboyant, but rather safer than that of Mr Toad and more akin to that of Inspector Morse – was recently provided by a Penzance resident. In a letter to a *Daily Telegraph* motoring correspondent, he offered for sale a 1968 Jaguar 240, in excellent condition with only 41,000 miles on its clock, full service records and a year's tax and MOT.

As the editor of *Miller's Classic Cars Price Guide* has explained, 'indulgence' is a 'primary reason' for buying these particular vehicles, while 'a second motive is investment, combining the physical pleasure of driving a classic car with the comforting knowledge that it has been money well spent'. Like all things sometimes such an investment 'may prove a poor decision' but then again a profit may accrue later 'when prices have changed' through changes in fashion and the economic climate.

As financial advisers Towry Law indicated in one of their client updates published in 2000, the recession of the early 1990s saw a 'sharp decrease in the value of art and antiques'. However, in the new millennium, 'we are now witnessing a steady increase in values approaching and, in some cases, exceeding the high levels seen in the late 1980s'. Then Robin Duthy was able to chronicle some steady and impressive investment returns. Today, encouragingly, Towry Law report something of a price recovery, with a rise in the value of antiques 'right across the board. For example, Studio glass and pottery, Edwardian and twentieth-century furniture and works of art have all increased in value'.

As so many investors in tangibles are fond of stressing, things work for the best when pleasure in possessing them is accompanied by a well-founded expectation that they are appreciating significantly in value while this pleasure is being experienced. However, what some would-be acquirers of pleasure-giving artefacts may not appreciate is that, in the eloquent words of compulsive collector, Charles Paget Wade:

collecting gives such a wonderful opportunity for a wider view of humanity . . . how varied are the traits of those met with when searching for 'finds' . . . to how many interesting strange, out-of-the-way places collecting has led – to old cities, markets, sleepy country towns, peaceful remote country villages at home and abroad.

The prospect of such enjoyable travelling around in search of tangibles does much to induce some early leavers to look to these alternative investments, not only to provide possible profit but also considerable pleasure.

KEY ADVICE

■ Consider investing in tangible, non-paper investments that provide pleasure in ownership, as well as increases in value over time.
■ Remember that such investments may take time to convert back to cash, if this is required or advised.
■ Contact Art Market Research, 83 Stoke Newington Church Road, London N16 0AS (Tel. 0208 968 9900) for data on the recent investment track records of various tangibles and collectibles. Alternatively, log on to www.artindex.co.uk.

■ Seek specialist advice before purchasing any tangible as an investment.
■ Consider investing in vintage champagne, mature claret or old whisky, but before doing so seek specialist advice. Note that trading in wine is possible via two websites:
www.uvine.com
www.winebid.com
■ Get updates on the prices of works of art and antiques by logging on to www.christies.com or from the Auction Channel at www.auctionchannel.com

18
Assessing the risks of investments

If you can look into the seeds of time,
And say which grain will grow and which will not,
Speak then to me
Macbeth, Act I

OVERVIEW

As an early leaver, your investment capital is precious. In this final chapter you will learn about a scoring system you can use to assess and compare the risk associated with the various investments discussed earlier in this book.

When Barings Bank, previously trusted by many pillars of the establishment as a fit repository for their investment capital, collapsed early in 1995, the chairman of Barclays Bank was not alone in immediately checking whether his bank had adequate defences against any similar threat to its well being. This was rather appropriate, for at that very time a leaflet entitled *Your Guide to Investment Risk* could be found in many Barclays branches.

This guide could serve as a useful starting point for early retired investors who, like the chairman of Barclays, are wisely concerned about risk and seek to make sure they are comfortable with the degree to which they are exposed to it. Like some other instruments for personal financial assessment, the guide invites readers to identify with various distinct types of investor who it categorises according to their attitude to risk.

The most conservatively inclined is defined as a 'no-risk' investor – one 'averse to any downward fluctuations in accumulated value whatsoever', who, moreover, 'fully understands and accepts that, over the long term, the accumulated value [of an investment] is likely to be lower than investments in stocks and shares and may suffer from the effects of inflation' but who, nevertheless, 'prefers the security of a deposit-based savings account'.

By comparison, a 'low-risk' investor is defined as 'one prepared to see a limited degree of fluctuation in the value of the accumulated fund, in return for the likely prospect of a moderately higher return', while the much more typical 'medium-risk' investor is described as 'prepared to see a greater degree of fluctuation in the value of the accumulated fund in return for the prospect of a higher level of return'.

Finally comes the 'high-risk' investor, who is 'prepared to commit a significant proportion of his or her disposable income to stocks and shares and to place little emphasis on the short-term security of cash-based deposits'. Such an individual, in the view of Barclays, 'will probably have a good understanding of the stockmarket and may well be seeking investments that carry a higher risk/reward profile than other more conservative ones. For example, this type of investor may already hold, or be prepared to invest in, specialist unit trusts, individual company shares, etc. etc.'

Because the early retired are likely to receive smaller occupational and state pensions than those of statutory retirement age, and are unlikely, if they also have a private pension, to want initially to draw on this at 55 or very soon after, they should do all they can to ensure that the capital they can spare for investment is not involved in risky speculation. Fortunately, to help them achieve this, two widely-respected investment experts, David Aaron and Margaret Stone (author of perhaps the clearest and most succinct book on saving early retirers can acquire, the Daily Mail's annual *Savers' Guide*), have each adopted a scoring system to assess the risks of various investments. These include the investments this book has recommended early retirers to discuss with their financial advisers. When Aaron's risk ratings – which can be found in his excellent *What Investment* magazine supplement 'Investing for Income' – are combined with Stone's – found in her Daily Mail guide – out of a possible (perhaps rather crudely) combined 'maximum security' rating of 15, Guaranteed Income Bonds and non-index-linked gilts (held to maturity) scored 15, bank and building society deposits

Risk and reward

The following diagram gives an indication of the varying levels of risk involved with varying types of investment. Even riskier investments, e.g. warrants and futures, are excluded.

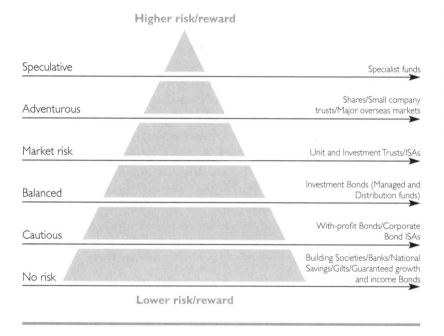

Higher risk/reward

Speculative	Specialist funds
Adventurous	Shares/Small company trusts/Major overseas markets
Market risk	Unit and Investment Trusts/ISAs
Balanced	Investment Bonds (Managed and Distribution funds)
Cautious	With-profit Bonds/Corporate Bond ISAs
No risk	Building Societies/Banks/National Savings/Gilts/Guaranteed growth and income Bonds

Lower risk/reward

Source: Hargreaves Lansdown

and index-linked gilts 13, With Profits Bonds 11 and Distribution Bonds and Unit and Investment Trust ISAs 10.

In scoring from between 15 and 10 points on this scale, many of the investments for early leavers discussed in detail in earlier chapters entail only non-existent, low or medium levels of risk (see the figure above). This, of course, is as it should be. The investment capital available to many early retirers is precious and so should be put to work in ways that are essentially safe, as well as potentially productive.

KEY ADVICE

▪ As an early retirer, involve yourself only in investments that carry low or medium risk to the vital capital you have available.

▪ Take comfort in the fact that many investments of possible interest to the early retirer – such as guaranteed income bonds, index-linked and non-index linked gilts, bank and building society deposits, with profits bonds, distribution bonds, and some unit and investment trust ISAs – are not generally considered to involve high risk.

Postscript

By now it should have become clear to you that, like all great things, the Great Escape of early retirement is likely to succeed only after some effort. Not all this effort is expended during a full-time working career and some of it requires prudent foresight, careful planning and shrewd investing before, as well as after, this career ends.

With the erosion of state support during retirement likely to increase in the future, it is even more incumbent on all who wish to retire early, both in the near but especially in the more distant future, to supplement occupational and state schemes by making their own private superannuation arrangements. Fortunately, the arrival of stakeholder pensions and the regular discussion nowadays of various pensions issues has prompted many to pull their heads out of the sand. Starting as early as their twenties, these people are charting well-planned courses that can realistically be expected to enable them to leave work early.

Pressure and stress on workers in this new century are both likely to increase as the century proceeds. It is likely that increasing numbers will want or may have to leave full-time jobs prematurely.

Leaving your job early can potentially, and often does actually, become a Great Escape. The experience of redeploying your skills and reorienting your efforts can bring about what in your later years amounts to a reinvention of yourself. These years then become an exciting and fulfilling finale to the many previous ones spent, happily or not, in full-time employment.

Appendix I
Pensions in detail

Types of pension

State Pension

State provision consists of the Basic State Pension and the State Earnings Related Pension Scheme (SERPS).

Basic State Pension

The full basic State Pension is currently £72.50 a week for a single person, or £115.90 for a married couple. To qualify for the full pension, you must have made National Insurance contributions for a minimum of 44 years for men and currently, in normal circumstances, 39 years for women. Men may claim the Basic State Pension from the age of 65. However, women born from 1955 onwards will not be able to claim the Basic State Pension until they reach the age of 65. For certain circumstances there will be transitional arrangements which your financial adviser will be able to explain to you.

State Earnings Related Pension Scheme (SERPS)

You will be eligible for some SERPS pension at State Pension age if, at any time since 1978, you have been an employee earning above the Lower Earnings Level (LEL) and were not 'contracted out', either through a personal pension or a company scheme. (NB If you are contracted out of SERPS, make sure that the relevant National Insurance rebates have been properly applied to your particular pension plan.) The actual SERPS pension you will receive will be based on your average earnings in the years you were a member. For someone retiring today who has been a member continually since 1978 the maximum benefit is £5642.

You should ask your local office of the Department of Social Security to provide an estimate of any SERPS pension you are entitled to receive. Do remember that these benefits can not be taken before State Pension age, so you might need to make other plans to support yourself up to then.

Occupational pension schemes

As Toby Walne recently pointed out in the *Daily Telegraph*, 'anyone with an opportunity of joining a company pension scheme should generally jump at the chance' because 'employers generally put in extra money in line with wage contributions'. Moreover, an occupational pension is extremely tax-efficient in that it 'offers relief up to the 40 per cent tax bracket and allows you to put in up to 15 per cent of earnings'. As Walne further points out, 'employers typically put £20 into your pension for every £10 contributed from your own pocket'! What is more, you can top up your 'works' pension scheme by making Additional Voluntary Contributions (AVCs) to it, or supplement it via entirely separate private additional arrangements you make with an insurance company of your choice, in the form of Free Standing Additional Contributions (FVACs).

Occupational pension schemes come in two types. The first, commonly but not exclusively applicable to public service employees, is the 'final salary' or 'defined benefit' scheme. This promises to pay a proportion of your final salary when you retire for each year that you have been a member. Typically, a scheme might pay one-sixtieth of your final salary for each year of service up to a maximum of 40 years, to give a maximum pension of two-thirds of your final salary. However, you should note that some schemes are less generous than this and that most employees do not, in fact, serve for as long as 40 years. The second type of occupational pension is the 'defined contribution' scheme, which also offers good value for savings and is becoming increasingly common. It is tied to the amount of money put into it over the years to build an individual 'pot' of money on retirement. According to present, but increasingly unpopular, legislation, this sum has to be used to buy an annuity, which will then provide you with an income for the rest of your life.

If you remain unsure which of these two occupational pensions you have, then simply ask your employer. It is also a good idea, if appropriate, for you to contact your previous employers to check whether you were in either of these two occupational pension schemes. They will be able to give you an estimate of how much you might eventually receive as a result of this historic involvement. You can also contact the Pensions Scheme Registry, PO Box 1NN, Newcastle-upon-Tyne, NE99 1NN 9, Tel. 0191 225 6316 to trace any previous scheme membership.

A further point made in the government information leaflet on pensions (from which some of this introductory information has been gleaned), is fairly obvious to prospective early leavers but nonetheless worth reiterating. It is the reminder that 'if you want to retire earlier than the scheme pension age, any pension you may receive may be less than if you retired at the scheme pension age'. The word 'may' is correct here, because enhancement incentives could allow an early retirer to receive as much by way of a 'works' pension as they would eventually receive if taking statutory retirement at 65!

Obviously, any prospective Great Escapee into early retirement should find out exactly how much less will be received if early, as opposed to statutory, retirement is taken. But whenever you receive a projection of what your pension will be, as Barclays Bank has counselled, 'don't forget to account for the effects of inflation'. For instance, allowing for an inflation rate of 2.5 per cent per annum, a figure of £30,000 in 30 years' time would have the same buying power as £14,300 today. Also remember that salaries tend to increase faster than inflation!

So far pensions have been described – state and occupational ones – that everyone has to join or many get the beneficial chance to do so. However, there are other superannuation arrangements which involve greater degrees of freedom and personal choice.

Choosing a pension

Your choice of a pension is limited in many respects because it depends on your occupational status. If you work for a firm which provides you with a pension, you are classed for tax purposes as a Schedule D employee and the firm's pension involved can be contributory or non-contributory. If you wish to supplement whatever arrangement is made, you can made AVCs or entirely separate FSAVCs, which means you fund premiums into your own choice of pension arrangements. Usually, FSAVCs are less cost effective than AVCs which, it should be noted, can only be made to occupational pension schemes. However, FSAVCs do offer a flexible investment opportunity. The contracts they involve can be deferred to await improved annuity rates, even if the main scheme benefits are already 'in payment', and changing jobs (unlike the situation with AVCs) does not involve transfer penalties because an FSAVC is tied to the individual rather than the employer. Finally, FSAVCs, unlike AVCs, provide benefits that do not have to be taken at the same time as main scheme benefits.

If you are in non-pensionable employment – you either work for a firm that does not provide a pension, or are self-employed – there are two superannuation options available. The first is to make your own private arrangements via a personal pension provider or, if you are able to make an annual premium contribution of £25,000 or a single contribution of £50,000, to take out what is known as a Self Invested Personal Pension or SIPP (see more below). If you are a director of a thriving (if small) business you can take advantage of pension arrangements that can operate as tax-saving vehicles. Huge premiums can often be funded into these executive pension arrangements and the controlling directors involved have the choice of either funding into a proprietary scheme or having their own Small Self-Administered Scheme or SSSA, the funding levels for which differ from those governing 'standard' personal pension arrangements.

The choice of a pension is a difficult and complex business. However, the editor of Money Mail, Margaret Stone, has written a booklet sponsored by Commercial Union called *How to Choose a Personal Pension*, while the government has its own pensions website: www.pensions.gov.uk. In general, though, your personal choice of pension may well depend on the amount of money you are willing or able to plough into it.

Employees who do not have the option of investing in an employer's occupational scheme, directors of companies who are not in pensionable employment (via, say, their own SSSA) and also the self-employed who can afford to invest 'serious' money of at least £15,000 or more per annum into private pension arrangements, should all seriously consider an SIPP. Investing in a SIPP to the tune of just £2,000 or £3,000 per annum would almost certainly be bad value, while to be really viable, this particular pension product requires annual contributions of £25,000 or £50,000 as a single contribution. In some circumstances it may prove more expensive to fund than many run-of-the-mill, standard personal pensions, but it is likely to prove more lucrative and in any case the costs incurred tend not to vary with the size of the contributions made. Every SIPP is distinctive in that each consists of a diversified investment portfolio in a pensions 'wrapper'. A. J. Bell, IPS trustees, Suffolk Life and Hargreaves Lansdown are three firms that can provide a pension 'shell' to wrap around such a portfolio, the particular constituents of which are selected by a broker.

As Hargreaves Lansdown explain in their SIPP leaflet, the flexibility and choice of permitted investments make a SIPP an extremely attractive product. To me it seems ideally suited to intelligent early retirement planning by the better-off. Its structure allows both for regular contributions or one-off lump sum payments, as these become possible. Very advantageously too, a SIPP can be viable until an annuity has to be purchased, currently by the age of 75. Experts see the SIPP's major strength as the variety of its permitted constituents, which can comprise cash deposits, UK gilts (or other fixed-interest securities), stocks and shares (quoted on the UK or other recognised overseas stock markets), unit trusts, open-ended investment companies (OEICs), investment trusts, managed funds from insurance companies (TIPs) and commercial property. In other words, the would-be early retirer who can afford a SIPP can resort to a plethora of potent tools with which to dig an escape tunnel!

If you wish to take out this type of pension you can choose one of a number of 'off the peg' but carefully tailored, though not exactly 'bespoke', portfolios that should really suit your needs as an early retirer. A further advantage of this arrangement is that it absolves SIPP holders from any need to make their own investment decisions.

As Hargreaves Lansdown point out in their guide, tax relief at the highest marginal rate is available on the premiums paid into the SIPP. The assets accumulate in a very tax-efficient way so that on maturity, this rather specialised and subtle pension provides a tax-free lump sum of the benefits that have accrued. You will have to pay for initially setting up a SIPP, for annual administration and for dealing in stocks and shares. You will also have to pay charges that are made for property transactions on a time-costed basis.

To my mind, the sheer variety of transactions involved in this particular 'pension-wrapped' investment make holding it as exciting as playing Monopoly – except that you have the very real prospect of making substantial profits by the time the game is over! Most advantageously, this need not be until your seventy-fifth birthday. Crucially, before then you can both preserve and manage the investments in your SIPP portfolio in what Hargreaves Lansdown rightly describes as a 'most efficient and transparent manner'.

The table opposite shows how the amount you are allowed to contribute varies over the years. This makes an SIPP a well-spread, well-balanced, particularly tax-efficient investment that, especially over the long term, has very good prospects of proving lucrative. It offers the high-earning prospective early leaver an escape route whose ingenuity and sound construction, based on intelligent planning, provide a model for other less affluent escapees.

As will now be clear, there are pretty specific guidelines on how much you can put into a pension plan. This depends on what is known as 'net relevant earnings': the income you receive from employment, excluding investment income.

Age at beginning of tax year (6 April)	Percentage of net relevant earnings that you may contribute in any one tax year
16–35	17.5
36–45	20.0
46–50	25.0
51–55	30.0
56–60	35.0
61–74	40.0

Source: Hargreaves Lansdown

If you have between £5000 and £10,000 per annum to invest in a private pension, the SIPP route will prove too expensive. Paying into a more conventional and less complex private pension that taps into many top-performing and diverse funds run by specialist managers would make better sense. In this connection, the name Skandia Life is worth considering. This insurance company, unlike so many others, does not offer access only to the single, possibly mediocre, 'house wine' of its own pension fund, which could well be inferior to many rivals. Instead, Skandia offer a much more extensive 'wine list' of 200 possible funds from which early retirers can choose ten. This enables them to place their private pension contributions in a way that can really satisfy and sustain them. Other providers of pension products through which the pension holder can plump for widespread diversity are Merchant Investors and Winterthur. Like Skandia these tap into many independent funds.

For the majority who have incomes that are good enough but cannot compare with those necessary to fund SIPPs or 'fund of funds' arrangements like the Skandia scheme, there is a wide choice of plans available. These now include stakeholder pensions, which will be discussed in more detail shortly. Before then it seems sensible to consider features, other than the cost of the contributions required and the charges involved, that the prospective purchaser of a 'single company' private pension should consider.

An ABC guide to these features would start with the terms 'accommodating and adaptable'. The former relates to the plan's ability to absorb any other pension funds that have accrued from previous employment (provided, of course, that your pension advisers recommend this as the best option). The latter applies if the pension can take account of the changing circumstances of the pension holder, who may, for example, have to stop making contributions for a period but then wish to restart them.

A personal pension is said to be 'companionable' if it allows your employer to contribute to it; examples of such an arrangement are some newly introduced stakeholder schemes. Pension plans are 'convertible' if, like cars whose hoods can be rolled back in warm weather, they have a feature that can come into play to suit those who find themselves enjoying sunny days – such as financial high fliers able to bask in their good fortune!

If a pension is 'divisible', not all of it need be taken at any one time but, rather, only a proportion of it. If say, you take a part-time job, as commonly is the case in early retirement, the income from this plus a portion of your private pension can enable you to ease your way into retirement 'proper'. 'Encashable' means a proportion – often 25 per cent – of what a pension generates on maturity can be taken as a tax-free lump sum, while 'expandable' applies to any provision in a plan that allows increases in contributions to be made at any time.

Until recently, being 'flexible' meant the benefits of a private pension could be enjoyed at any time over the age of 50. However, in the summer of 2000, the Government announced that this goalpost would be moved backwards to 55. 'Immediate' is a description that can be applied to a personal pension that does not specify any qualifying period in which contributions cannot be made, while 'investment-orientated' (a term which, like many others discussed here was the inspired concoction of Margaret Stone) is a key feature that means that a scheme involves a wide range of investments likely to produce very acceptable returns.

For fairly obvious reasons, analysts use the term 'modern' to describe products that can accommodate contemporary developments in the lives of working pension payers (such as contract working, for example) or which reflect fresh or innovative thinking regarding these products themselves. A private pension is said to be 'moveable' if it allows for changed timescales – for example, one caused by deferring the time at which an annuity will have to be purchased from the proceeds of the matured pension. This term may also be used if, though only on professional advice, a pension can reasonably smoothly and none too expensively be transferred into a replacement plan.

A very desirable, but understandably far from cheap, 'protective' pension plan has the advantage that contributions to it will continue to be made if you fall ill or become unable to work. Finally, and most importantly, a plan is 'tax-efficient' if contributions made to it receive tax relief at the highest marginal rate of tax.

It may have become apparent to you that stakeholder pensions possess many of the desirable features of private pensions just outlined. Indeed, these relatively new products have been described as the 'low-cost alternative' to existing private pension schemes. As well as being low cost, they are essentially flexible, being subject to the following investor-friendly rules:

The basic rules that every stakeholder pension will have to meet:

- The minimum contribution you can make will be £20 or less.
- There is no minimum frequency with which you will have to contribute.
- You will be able to transfer the whole of your pension fund out of a stakeholder plan to a new stakeholder pension plan at no cost.
- There is no initial cost to invest, meaning that 100 per cent of your money is invested into your pension fund. If you make a single contribution of £1000, then £1000 will be invested into your pension fund.
- There are no penalties if you change your contribution or retirement age, or if you wish to stop payments.
- There can only be one charge on the plan and this is a percentage of the fund value each year. This cannot be any higher than 1 per cent.
- Individual financial advice is not included in this cost.

Source: Hargreaves Lansdown

As Hargreaves Lansdown point out in *A One Minute Guide to Stakeholder Pensions*, unlike many other financial products, stakeholder pensions are easy to compare because there is only one charge on the contract. One major advantage of stakeholder plans is that contributors to them do not have to be high earners. Another is that plans are available to the many millions who already have occupational pensions but earn less than £30,000 a year. This concession is of particular value to young workers who want to make long-term plans for early retirement. The permitted levels of contributions to stakeholder pensions exactly match those for SIPPs set out in the table above. To clarify the question of how much can be put into a stakeholder, Hargreaves Lansdown have provided the following information:

How much can I put into a stakeholder?

■ There is no link between earnings and the amount you can contribute to a stakeholder if your contributions are £3600 or less each year
■ This means that you do not have to have any earned income to pay up to £3600 into a stakeholder pension every year.
■ All contributions will be made net of basic rate tax, for the employed, self-employed and non workers. An investment of £780 will result in £1000 in your pension fund, after basic rate tax has been claimed.
■ For contributions above £3600 a year you do have to have an earned income and the amount you can contribute is restricted to Inland Revenue limits.

Source: Hargreaves Lansdown

In general, when you are considering as one of the main financial planks of your escape tunnel not which private pension to purchase but how much to contribute to it, you should bear in mind two rather sobering recommendations. The first is that, according to conventional wisdom, you should invest between 10 and 15 per cent of your income into a pension if you want a retirement fund of 50 per cent of your current earnings – and the sooner the better (Weekend Money in *The Times*, 9 September 2000). The second comes from Anne Ashworth, the editor of Weekend Money. In her view, to live well in what she calls your declining years (I prefer to call it 'life's longest holiday'), while in work you should save the proportion of your income that is equivalent to half your current age.

Monitoring and optimising your superannuation arrangements

As with your medical health, you should periodically monitor your financial health. An essential part of this is the state of your super-annuation arrangements.

If you are a member of a final salary scheme, you can ask for the details of your present position and projections of the benefits you may receive on the date of your early (or later) retirement. Sometimes the calculation of what you will have accrued by the possible date for your early retirement becomes the starting point for inviting employees to leave their jobs prematurely. Antonia Senior noted in a recent article in the *Daily Telegraph* that members of money purchase scheme should receive not just annual benefit statements but also details of investment performance, because that is what the annual benefits will rely on. Personal pension providers should also furnish regular statements. The Department of Social Security in Newcastle-upon-Tyne will provide, on receipt of form BR 19, an exact 'state of play' forecast of the amount of State Retirement Pension you will receive if (a) full National Insurance contributions continue to be made until statutory retirement, and (b) if such contributions were to cease at some stipulated (early retirement) point before that date.

If you are dissatisfied with the management of an occupational or personal pension, it is best, in the first instance, to contact its administrator. If you still are not satisfied, get in touch with the Occupational Pensions Advisory Service (OPAS), Tel. 020 7233 6393.

If you (like so many people contacted by the television programme *Find a Fortune* have, in changing jobs, lost track of benefits preserved in a previous superannuation scheme to which you no longer contribute, contact the Pension Schemes Registry (Tel. 0191 225 6393). While they are not able to trace such benefits, they may be able to put you on their trail. Finally, in cases of great dissatisfaction, there is the Pensions Ombudsman who, unlike the OPAS, can adjudicate in legally binding ways.

As for the equally important task of monitoring the performance of your pension fund(s), you can do much of this yourself by reading magazines such as *Pensions World* or *What Pension* and studying the information pension specialists can provide.

Taking non-state pensions

From comments already made it will have become clear that there are many ways and times when you can do this. If you are in a final salary or company scheme, you have no choice: you have to take what your pension arrangements stipulate and provide for.

However, if you have funded your pension yourself through an executive scheme (SSAS) or a personal pension, or if (like me) historically you have taken out what the tax authorities style a Section 226 pension (which gives a lump sum of up to three times the starting income, roughly 22–30 per cent of the fund) various options are available. One is to 'commute' some of your pension to provide a tax-free lump sum – a good idea if you have dependents or beneficiaries, because then the benefits will not die with you!

There are several reasons why taking a pension is a complex and complicated business. One is the unfortunate fact that rates for compulsory annuities (the actual pension you buy) are very low. Indeed, this is why Equitable Life, who made historic guarantees of higher ones, has recently found itself hoist with its own petard!

However, there are some beneficial ways whereby accrued pension 'pots' can be converted into investments that are managed to produce income yet keep the capital well-preserved. These can involve arrangements known as 'Phased Retirement' and 'Pension Fund Withdrawal', also referred to as 'Income Drawdown' – to which Hargreaves Lansdown has provided informative guides and succinct summaries. One such is given opposite.

If you have an adequate fund – Hargreaves Lansdown suggest £100,000 – you can, as an alternative, have what is known as a 'drawdown' pension. This has a number of advantages and one possible disadvantage.

You can start with a low level of income from your pension and increase it as your needs increase. What you are actually doing via this arrangement is investing your pension for maximum growth and drawing chunks of it as income.

Alternatively, you can (according to current tax rules, which may change however) pass the value of your drawdown pension to your beneficiaries. Otherwise, if by the time of your death you had actually bought a compulsory annuity from the proceeds of a maturing pension, this would die with you. Currently too, you can keep a drawdown pension until the age of 75 but legislation to extend this limit is expected. In effect, with a drawdown pension your fund operates in the way an employment pension scheme operates in that the pool of money available is invested to pay out the pension.

Phased retirement (also known as staggered vesting)

This is a consideration for more substantial funds, for instance over £100,000. Your pension fund is transferred into a phased retirement plan, which is split into (say) 1000 identical segments or clusters. It is then possible to take the benefits from each segment separately.

Each segment will provide a 25 per cent tax free cash sum, with the balance of the segment being used to buy an annuity. The segments are encashed as and when required, to provide a number of tax free cash payments and a series of annuities.

In the early years, tax free cash makes up the majority of the income, making it very tax efficient. Phased retirement can be particularly attractive if you do not need all the tax free cash up front, or if, for example, you continue to work part time.

The remainder of the fund remains invested and will hopefully continue to grow. Any segments which remain invested can normally be returned to your beneficiaries free of Inheritance Tax on your death. For this reason, death benefits are more attractive than those available under a conventional annuity.

Phased retirement provides an increase in flexibility. You can encash segments of the plan to provide income when required. However, this does not solve the problem of poor annuity rates. You do have to take the risk that annuity rates may fall, meaning that any growth on the fund may not compensate for the income you would have received, had you taken out a conventional annuity on day one.

This type of arrangement has higher charges than those associated with a conventional annuity.

Source: Hargreaves Lansdown

However, there is a possible disadvantage to the drawdown scheme. An occupational plan's administrating actuary, rather like the fireman of a steam locomotive, monitors and 'stokes' the fund to ensure it can achieve a head of financial 'steam' sufficient for it to meet its potential liabilities in the future. As a further means of ensuring this happens, like the driver of the locomotive, the actuary has a hand constantly on the controls, regularly adjusting the amount the employer pays in. By contrast, the holder of a drawdown pension has no chance to fine-tune its funding, and so must gamble that the way its controls were initially set will actually produce a pension that is higher than if an annuity had been bought straightaway on retirement.

Several points made above are worth reiterating or amplifying. One is that eventually, although this can be deferred until you are 75, you have to purchase an annuity when your private pension matures. This is when you should contact specialist annuity

---

Pension Fund Withdrawal (also known as Income Drawdown)

This type of arrangement is a consideration for more substantial funds, for instance, over £100,000.

With this kind of policy, the pension fund is transferred to a special type of contract, where it is possible to withdraw income directly from the fund. You can withdraw income from the fund up to the age of 75, when you have to buy an annuity with the remaining fund. The advantage of this type of plan is that you can control your income requirements, whilst continuing to actively manage the remaining fund.

The amount of income you can take from the fund each year is subject to strict Inland Revenue limits. The maximum is roughly equivalent to the income you would receive from a single life, level annuity at that time. The minimum you can take is 35 per cent of the maximum. These limits are set by the Government Actuary Department, and are known as GAD limits. These limits are recalculated every three years.

It is possible to take the maximum tax-free cash at outset. Any further income is then counted as taxable income. However, because you can control how much income you take, and when you take it, you can structure your income payments to minimise your tax liability.

The remainder of the fund remains invested. Any growth is free from any liability to capital gains tax. Withdrawals can continue to be made until age 75.

The death benefits from Pension Fund Withdrawal are often more attractive than those available with a conventional annuity.

Source: Hargreaves Lansdown

advisers and arrangers such as Hargreaves Lansdown or Towry Law (who can provide a guide), Annuity Solutions, Bridegate Annuities, Annuity Direct or the Annuities Bureau. Of these firms, the first publishes a leaflet entitled *Other Types of Annuity*, a booklet on 'with-profit' and 'unit-linked' annuities. They can conduct an annuity search for a client who has finally, or been advised to, purchase this traditionally rather staid and safe product, which to some may still have a somewhat Dickensian ring! Sadly, if this annuity is purchased in a 'standard', less-sophisticated form than the two versions described above, and rather lazily from the same company as pays out your maturing pension, you may find yourself, if not quite as badly strapped as Mr Micawber, then stuck with quite paltry returns for the rest of your life!

Fortunately, help and advice from the above annuity specialists should prevent this. Hargreaves Lansdown has revealed the little-known and to some perhaps surprising fact that, by declaring health problems (even some seemingly minor ones) you could increase for the rest of your days your retirement income from an annuity. As Hargreaves Lansdown put it, 'if you were to apply for life assurance, these factors may count against you, but the good news is that when you come to retirement, these factors may actually help you to get an enhanced annuity rate!' Amazingly, it is 'estimated that 40 per cent of people could qualify for enhanced rates, yet only a tiny proportion actually apply for them'.

Significantly both Edmund Tirbutt (in a recent article in *Financial Mail on Sunday*) and Hargreaves Lansdown draw attention to the possibility of purchasing a non-standard (since non-flat rate) annuity – a product known as a 'with-profits' annuity. In his article Tirbutt cites consultant Hugh Lachan's scepticism about the chances that currently very low annuity rates will improve much in the near future. However, 'because long-term interest rates are projected to remain low and this will mean low gilt yields' (on which flat-rate annuities are so reliant), Lachan sees with-profits annuities as offering 'some way' of escaping low fixed rates. These annuities, of course need not be bought from the provider of your pension. They involve the pensioner initially receiving an annual bonus rate of up to 5 per cent (occasionally 5½ per cent) and, if this rate is exceeded by the bonus rate declared, income rises by the difference between the two. However, Tirbutt notes that if 'bonus rates are lower than the anticipated rate income falls accordingly'.

As Tirbutt further comments 'there is generally little to choose between a with-profits and a fixed-rate annuity at the outset, but the client will benefit if bonus rates turn out to be better than the anticipated ones'. Tirbutt's fairly bullish assessment is echoed by Hargreaves Lansdown, who perceptively point out that few professional investment portfolio managers would invest solely in gilts for 25 years, which many holders of fixed-rate annuities will, in effect, commit themselves to doing. Instead, Hargreaves Lansdown urge those who have to purchase an annuity at least to consider a with-profits variant, because this (and an alternative unit-linked product) have been designed to provide an income that will increase over the years, in line with the growth of the with-profits or selected fund of the annuity provider. 'As always, there is an increased risk in exchange for potential growth', but, given currently very low 'flat' annuity rates and the danger that the payments these product could, like all forms of fixed income, be eroded by inflation, it does seem understandable that about three-quarters of all who nowadays consult annuity specialists eventually decide to avoid standard annuities.

Appendix II
Women and pension planning

Women often have several gaps in their 'reckonable' service, some caused by periods of unsuperannuated part-time work, others by years spent serving unpaid the needs of others. So they may in retirement find themselves with large holes in the two retirement umbrellas provided by, the state pension and income occupational pension arrangements. It may well be that these pensions are all, or almost all, they have to cover them financially over retirements that tend to last considerably longer than those of males.

To be entitled to a full state pension (whose value in any case is likely to continue to fall over time), they must have worked for 39 years and have paid full National Insurance contributions over that time. Moreover, to receive any state pension at all, these contributions must have been made for at least ten years. This second but little-known requirement is a compelling reason why women should obtain form BR 19 from the Department of Social Security in Newcastle-upon-Tyne, fill it in and return it. They will then find out how much or how little the National Insurance contributions they have paid will entitle them to on retirement. More importantly, if the state pension forecast they receive shows worrying shortfalls in income, these may in part, if not completely, be made good before it is too late, thanks to an official concession. This allows you to make a maximum of six years' worth of National Insurance back contributions in a one-off lump sum payment. Such a back payment can amount to a very worthwhile 'additional voluntary contribution' to the state pension scheme.

Many women assume that the men in their lives will make, if they have not already made, arrangements for their financial welfare in their autumn-tinted but certainly not always blue-rinsed, final years. While divorce is more common in the UK than in other European countries, fortunately it now poses less of a threat to women whose financial well-being in part depends on their spouse's pension arrangements. Becoming widowed can obviously bring financial problems to a married women, but even worse and more worrying can be the plight of a woman who loses a partner to whom she is not married, because his depleted pension benefits have no transfer value to her.

It is a disturbing fact that while more than 70 per cent of women are employed or self-employed, only 22 per cent of these women have made adequate provision for their own retirement!

If as a woman you are an independent earner and want to retire early, it is imperative that you take action as early in your working life as possible. While you can, and for as long as you can, you should:

1 Maximise your contributions to any non-stakeholder occupational pension schemes available to you.
2 Take out, again as early in your working life as possible, a private pension, possibly a stakeholder one. Either make your own arrangements or contribute to an employer-arranged stakeholder scheme. Continue to pay as much into these as possible, especially if you spend any periods away from full-time employment.
3 Protect your entitlement to the basic state pension by narrowing or closing gaps in your reckonable National Insurance contribution record. This can be expensive. For example, as Joanna Slaughter has pointed out, if a twenty-five-year-old takes a five-year career break, she will need to pay out 50 per cent more in National Insurance contributions than a man of similar age.

Note though that high-earning women who have already made fairly substantial payments into self-arranged personal pensions by the time they take career breaks are in a stronger position. They could find that their particular pension is flexible enough to accommodate quite smoothly such changes and subsequent moves back into employment.

If any more are needed, the following facts should provide further sobering reminders that pension provision is a matter to which many more women would be well advised to direct their full attention!

■ Too many women have made a worryingly small number of National Insurance contributions, and/or do not have a private pension, and/or have not yet entered an occupational pension scheme.
■ Even if women have been in full-time work throughout their working lives, they are likely to receive much lower pensions than men, partly because of their lower salaries. Yet their life expectancy is a good deal longer!
■ According to the Department of Social security:
    (i)   The average value of a man's occupational pension is £50,000, compared to £7000 for women.
    (ii) There are around 150,000 divorces a year. Of these it is estimated that pension sharing, which involves the 'breadwinner's' retirement fund being divided to give each partner freedom to invest in their own pension plan, will benefit around 50,000 women.

The following schedule from London Life of a woman's life-stages draws attention to the various priorities that arise at different ages. It provides a final reminder of why achieving your own independent financial security is so important.

Lifestage priorities

Here is an example of how a woman's priorities may change through her life.

Age	Lifestage	Priority for finances
20s	Single or with partner	Instant access to cash Borrowing Savings Mortgage Building a home
30s	Career move Relocation Children Career break	Investment Savings Pensions Mortgage increase protection School fees
40s	Children growing up Divorce (possibly) Return to work	Investment Pensions Protection Savings School fees
50s	Early retirement Children in further education	Further education costs Investment Health insurance
60s	Retirement Widowhood Ill-health	Protection of capital Adequate level of income Providing for grandchildren Financing health care

There is no such thing as a 'typical' lifestyle for a woman, but this table illustrates the many priorities that can arise in a woman's varied life which make her own financial security so important

Source: London Life

Directory of concerns to contact

Advisory and Brokerage Service
Tel. 020 7405 8535

Aaron, David
Shelton House, Woburn Sands, Milton Keynes MK17 8PF
Tel. 01908 281544. www.aaron.co.uk
Financial adviser and author of guides on tax planning,
distribution bonds, with profit bonds, investing for income,
investing a lump sum etc.

Allenbridge Group plc
16 Bolton Street, London W1E 8UZ
Financial advisers and publishers of guides and analytical surveys.

Asset Risk Consultants
Tel. 01483 723573

Association of Investment Trust Companies (AITC)
Tel. 020 7431 5222. www.altc.co.uk

**The Association of Private Client Investment Managers
and Stockbrokers**
Tel. 020 7247 7080. www.apcims.co.uk

Association of Unit Trusts and Investment Funds (AUTIF)
Durrant House, 8–13 Chiswell Street, London EC1Y 4YY
Tel. 020 7831 0898. www.itsonline.co.uk
www.investmentsfunds.org
Publishers of factsheets on buying shares in investment companies
and on doing so to produce income.

Association of Solicitor Investment Managers
Tel. 01892 870065

Bates Investment Services
Upperbank House, Stoneythorpe, Horsforth, Leeds LSD18 BN4
Tel. 0800 0926 996. www.batesonline.com
Advisers, brokers and publishers of *Helping You Through the Financial Maze, Maximising Your Retirement Income* and other guides.

Berkeley St James Ltd
Berkeley House, 15 Bark St East, Bolton BL1 2BQ
Tel. 01204 531414
Retirement specialists and producers of *Investing in Retirement.*

Best Investment
Tel. 020 7321 0100. www.bestinvest.co.uk
Advisers and producers of comparative surveys of investments.

Chase de Vere Investments plc
2 Queen's Square, Bath BA1 2HD
Tel. 0845 609 2001. www.chasedevere.co.uk
Advisers and producers of comparative surveys of GIBS, ISAs, etc.

Chelsea Financial Services
St James' Hall, Moore Park Road, London SW6 2JS
Tel. 020 7384 7300

Consumers' Association
Tel. 020 7830 6000. www.which.net

Department of National Savings
Charles House, 375 Kensington High Street, London W14 8SD
www.nationalsavings.co.uk
Providers of savings and investment products. Explanatory literature in post offices.

Department of Social Security
Richmond House, 79 Whitehall, London SW1A 2NS
Providers of benefits (if appropriate). Literature explaining these is in local offices.

Faculty and Institute of Actuaries (FIA)
Tel. 020 7632 2100. www.actuaries.org.uk

Fiona Price and Partners
Tel. 0207 430 0366. www.fionaprice.co.uk
Advisers, especially but not exclusively, on financial matters affecting women and publishers of the *Shark Free Guide to Financial Advice*.

Fraser Smith
Tel. 0707 672 900
Fee-charging pensions consultants/reviewers.
Fraser Smith is now part of Towry Law.

Hargreaves Lansdown
Kendal House, 4 Brighton Mews, Clifton, Bristol BS8 2NX
Tel. 0177 990 9000. www.hargreaveslansdown.co.uk
Providers of a very wide range of services to investors and of publications of special interest to the early retired, including a discount directory and guide to ISAs, unit trusts and OEICS, guides to investment trusts, and zeros, *A One Minute Guide to Stakeholder Pensions*, *A Guide to Phased Retirement and Income Drawdown*, a SIPP leaflet and others describing *Options at Retirement*, an annuity search, and assistance with retirement planning.

Henderson Touche Remnant
3 Finsbury Avenue, London EC2M 2PA
Publishers of a *Guide to Split Capital Trusts*.

Homeowners Friendly Society Ltd
PO Box 94, Gardner House, Hornbeam Park Avenue, Harrogate, North Yorkshire HG2 8XE

Independent Professional Advisors Services Ltd
Alexander House, Shakespeare Road, London N3 1XW
Financial management consultants and publishers of the *Capital Investment Guide*.

Interactive Investor
www.iii.co.uk

Kleinwort Benson Investment Management
PO Box 191, 10 Fenchurch Street, London EC3M 3LB
Advisers and authors, in association with *Personal Finance* magazine, of a five-part *A–Z of Personal Finance.*

Legal and General
Temple Court, 11 Queen Victoria Street, London EC4N 4TP
Insurance-related products and publishers of information on retirement planning for women.

London Life
Spectrum, Bond Street, Bristol BS1 3AL
Insurance policy providers and publishers of *Options – Retirement Planning for Women.*

Matrix
Tel. 0117 976 9444. www.matrixgroup.co.uk
Can supply a list of six financial advisers in a particular postcode area.

Minet Consultancy Services Ltd
Minet House, 66 Prescot Street, London E1 8BU
Authors of *Financial Planning for Retirement* and *Mid-Career Financial Planning.*

National Federation of Independent Financial Advisers
PO Box 700, High Wycombe, Bucks HP13 7AY

National Register of Fee-Based Advisers
Greystoke Place, Fetter Lane, London EC4 1ND
List available from *Money Management* magazine.

Occupational Pensions Advisory Service
11 Belgrave Road, London SW1V 1RB
Stakeholder helpline 0845 601 2923

The Pensions Annuity Friendly Society
Tel. 020 7680 8960. www.pafs.co.uk

Pensions Scheme Registry
Tel. 0191 225 6393

Registrar of Pension Schemes
PO Box 1NN, Newcastle-upon-Tyne NE99 1NN

Society of Financial Advisers
Tel. 020 8989 8464. www.sofa.org

Standard and Poor's Ratings
www.standardpoor.co.com

The Unit Trust Information Service
Kingsway, London WC2B 6TD

The Times Financial Information Service
www.timesmoney.co.uk

The With Profits Bond Shop
Tel. 0115 958 7555

Torquil Clark
Tel. 0800 0561835. www.tqonline.co.uk
Pensions and investments advisers.

Towry Law
Western Road, Bracknell, Berkshire RG12 1TL
Tel. 01344 828000
Advisers and publishers of *Choices in Retirement* and several other
guides of considerable interest to early leavers.

TSB
PO Box 6000, Victoria House, Birmingham B1 1BZ
Publishers of *A Guide to Disclosure*.

UNITAS
9 Henderson Avenue, Scunthorpe, South Humberside DN15 7RH
Advisers, discount providers and publishers of financial
newsletters.

Young Ridgeway and Associates Ltd
10 Borelli Yard, Farnham, Surrey
Financial advisers and publishers of a brochure on financing
retirement.

Regulatory bodies

Building Societies Commission
15 Great Marlborough Street, London W1V 2AX

Chartered Association of Certified Accountants (ACCA)
29 Lincoln's Inn Fields, London WC2A 3EE

Financial Services Authority
Consumer helpline: 0845 606 1234
Leaflet line: 0800 917 3311
www.fsa.gov.uk

Institute of Actuaries, Staple Inn Hall
High Holborn, London WC1V 7QJ

Institute of Chartered Accountants in England and Wales (ICAEW)
Chartered Accountants Hall, Moorgate Place, London EC2P 2BJ

Ombudsmen

Banking Ombudsman
70 Grays Inn Road, London WC1X 8NB

Building Societies Ombudsman
Grosvenor Gardens House, 35–37 Grosvenor Gardens, London SW1X 7AW

Insurance Ombudsman
6 Frederick's Place, London EC2R 8BT

Pensions Ombudsman
11 Belgrave Place, London SW1V 1RB

PIA Ombudsman
1 London Road, London EC2Y 5EA

Personal Investment Authority (PIA)
3/4 Royal Exchange Buildings, London EC3V 3NL

Official leaflets to acquire

From Inland Revenue

To find your nearest office, look under 'Inland Revenue' in your local telephone book. Most offices are open to the public from Monday to Friday, 9.30 am to 4.00 pm; some are also open outside these hours.

IR41   *Income Tax and Jobseekers' Allowance* (JSA)

IR78   *Personal Pensions*. A guide for tax.

IR80   *Income Tax and Married Couples*

IR87   *Letting and Your Home*. Including the 'Rent a Room' scheme and letting your previous home when you live elsewhere.

IR110   *A Guide for People with Savings*

IR121   *Income Tax and Pensioners*

IR129   *Occupational Pension Schemes*. An introduction. More detailed information from The Pension Schemes Office, Inland Revenue, Yorke House, PO Box 62, Castle Meadow Road, Nottingham NG2 1BG. Tel. 0115 974 1670.

IR138   *Living or Retiring Abroad? A Guide to UK Tax on Your UK Income*

IR139   *Income from Abroad? A Guide to UK Tax on Overseas Income*

IR165   *The New Individual Savings Accounts* (ISA)

CGT1   *Capital Gains Tax*. An introduction.

PSO1   *Occupational Pension Schemes*

From the Benefits Agency

To find your nearest office, look under 'Social Security or Benefits Agency' in your local telephone book.

CA01   National Insurance Contributions for Employees.

CA02   National Insurance Contributions for Self-Employed People With Small Earnings

CA08   Voluntary Contributions.

CWL1   Starting Your Own Business?

CA12   Training for Further Employment and Your National Insurance Record

CA53   Information about National Insurance Contributions

NI38   Social Security Abroad.

Glossary

Access to capital   A feature of an investment whereby its encashment is a rapid and straightforward procedure. Money held in instant access bank accounts has this advantage.

Additional voluntary contributions (AVCs)   Extra contributions made voluntarily, quite separately and regularly into an occupational pension scheme. If appropriate, these should be seriously considered by prospective early leavers. There are two types: 'in-house' AVCs and 'free-standing' AVCs. The former are group products and benefit from economies of scale. Moreover, they are invariably better value than their free-standing counterparts (FSAVCs), which often involve high charges. However, with the recent introduction of stakeholder pensions, people earning less than £30,000 a year can contribute to company pensions as well as to stakeholder pensions, which can thus function as alternatives to AVCs.

Annuity   An insurance policy that provides an income for life and which must, by the very latest at 75 (if appropriate), be purchased from the proceeds of a maturing private pension. Professional advice should be sought about the irrevocable choice among various kinds of annuity: single; joint-life arrangements that involve one's spouse; plans with payments guaranteed for a certain period; inflation-linked schemes; an escalating annuity; an 'impaired life' variety that takes account of lifestyle factors such as smoking or medical problems; a standard 'level' arrangement or one that is 'with profits' or 'unit-linked'.

Annuity search   Service offered by an intermediary, broker or adviser whereby the annuity market is 'trawled' to find the annuity provider and type of product best suited to a particular person's needs.

Asset allocation   Arrangement within an investment portfolio whereby money is widely spread across many different investments – such as shares, bonds and cash deposits – and/or across markets in many parts of the world.

Bed and breakfast   Arrangement designed to deal with the ravages of Capital Gains Tax, whereby holdings in a sector likely to incur this tax are sold at the end of one tax year and then in the next purchased from another provider of products in this sector. You can also use an existing security with a capital gain and transfer the security into an ISA. As Peter Hargreaves has put it, 'if you have £7000 in a share with a huge capital gain in it, you can sell that share and re-buy it back in the ISA, to use your full year's ISA allowance and create a capital gain'.

Bed and spousing   Not a reference to sex within marriage, but to an arrangement whereby assets can be transferred to a spouse to use up his or her Capital Gains Tax allowance (currently £7500 p.a.). One partner sells an investment before 5 April (so ensuring the capital gains involved fall short of £7500) and the spouse buys it back 30 days later.

Best advice   Advice that is impartial and given by an adviser in the interests of the client being advised. One way of increasing your chances of getting it is to use the services of a fee-charging and appropriately regulated adviser.

Blue chip   Term describing shares of the largest and most stable concerns on the stock market.

Bond   A lump sum investment that, over a fixed period, pays a set rate of interest. Bonds are issued both by companies and governments. Generally, they are less volatile and, in the long term, give higher income returns than many stocks and shares. The term itself implies some sort of guarantee or degree or predictability about the return offered on fixed-interest securities.

Bonus rate   Rate of return paid by an insurance company on a With Profits policy.

'Buying in' of service An arrangement sometimes available with occupational pensions schemes which makes it possible retrospectively to purchase past years of pensionable service that were not superannuated at the time. This makes these years 'reckonable' and so to feature in calculations that will eventually determine the size of this pension. Sometimes, what would otherwise be 'proceeds-eroding' gaps in reckonable pension service can be bridged by retrospective payments made prior to early or statutory retirement.

Capital gains Any gains in value or profit made when an asset or investment is sold or otherwise disposed of.

Capital Gains Tax Tax on any such gains in value or profit. Currently, annual capital gains of less than £7500 are exempt from this tax.

Cash ISA The constituent of the Individual Savings Account that carries the least risk. It can serve as the repository of up to £1000 of a person's annual ISA allowance. Commonly a deposit account, it can also take the form of a money-market unit trust and function as a mini ISA. But if it does so, no more than £3000 p.a. can be invested in a stocks-and-shares ISA. If a cash ISA is part of a maxi ISA, any funds it does not absorb can be invested in the providing company's stocks-and-shares ISA. It is advisable to select a cash ISA which reaches the government's CAT standard by paying an interest rate of no less than 2 per cent below bank base rate, by accepting deposits as little as £1, and requiring no more than seven working days' notice of any withdrawals.

Credit rating Assessment given to a bond by a rating agency (such as Standard and Poor's) that takes account of its strength and likelihood of repaying capital. The best such rating is 'triple A' (AAA).

Cyber-account/cyberbank Internet-linked bank or building society account which can be highly competitive or even market-leading but which should be subject to checks on its safety and security.

Deposit Money lodged with a bank or building society in an account that is interest-bearing.

Derivatives Share-linked financial instruments. Some of the most popular are futures, options and warrants but investing in these is a specialised business (see Directory of concerns to contact for guides).

Disclosure   Process whereby financial advisers have to reveal the sizes and sources of any commissions they receive.

Discount broker   Intermediary who arranges an investment for a client. The latter can gain in that this agent does not take all of the commission due to him or her, but sacrifices some of it to benefit the investor. The commission will either by re-invested on behalf of the client in order to increase the size of the investment, or will be rebated by cheque. Failing to make an investment through a discount broker can involve the forfeiture of any chance to get back some of the commission it carries, because all of this will be kept back for itself by the investment provider!

Discounts   These are reductions on the costs of making investments and can be attractively large. The early leaver is thus advised to shop around between both investment providers and discount brokers. Other discounts for the early leaver involve age-related travel, leisure and insurance concessions. NB 'Discount' is also a specialised financial term used to indicate how the share price of an investment trust stands in relation to the assets of this trust. If the assets of such a trust were £1 per share and its shares traded at 90p, this would represent a 10 per cent discount.

Distribution bonds   Bonds issued by insurance companies that 'strip out' income from their investments and automatically pay it out to the bondholders. These bonds all involve money being placed in a mix of shares and bonds. Currently, this investment is less popular with many of the retired and with early leavers than With Profits bonds.

Downside risk   Expression that refers to the possibly disadvantageous, because potentially risky, implications and features of an investment. It is vital that this factor is considered as a 'devil's advocate's argument' before committing yourself to any investment.

Downsizing   Reduction of the scope or size of employment, lifestyle or living space (such as by moving to another smaller property). It is a common recourse of those leaving early or retiring at 65. However, too drastic a reduction in your stake in the property market is best avoided.

Drawdown   An insurance product that enables a personal pensions saver, if so advised, to defer purchase of an annuity until he or she is 75 and, until this age is reached, to enhance the funding or retirement by receiving a limited, but nonetheless very welcome, additional annual income. For this extra income to be large enough to be attractive, a private pension on maturity should have produced a 'pot' of at least £100,000. If less than this has accrued, any advantage would be offset by set-up and ongoing charges. Such charges are also high if you switch from one provider of this subtle financial arrangement to another.

The benefit to those in a financial position to profit from income drawdown is that it allows your pension to remain invested in the stockmarket where it can grow, while also allowing you to withdraw an income every year. Given increasing longevity, such an arrangement will hold for many who are suited to it for a good ten years, even if they take 'statutory' retirement!

Earnings cap   Ceiling limit on the total amount of an individual's annual earnings that can feature in calculations involving stipulated proportions of this income that each year can be paid into a private pension. Currently, for those under 35, such annual 'private-pension eligible' income is capped at £91,400. In essence, the earnings cap is an Inland Revenue threshold designed to prevent very high earners putting too much money into their own pensions, because contributions to these from above earnings above the cap receive no tax relief.

Escalator bond   Deposit bond whose distinguishing feature is that, by predetermined increments, the rate of interest increases each year. Rates in the early years tend to be low but enhanced rates may apply to large sums invested.

Equities   Shares.

Equity income   Income from investments involving shares.

Exit fees   Financial penalties charged for a premature exit from an investment, i.e. made before its previously stipulated full

and fixed term (or 'lifespan' as a valid investment) has
expired.

First option bonds National Savings product. These bonds
pay a rate of interest that is fixed for a year. When this period
has elapsed and on each and every subsequent 'birthday' of the
bonds held, the saver can encash them, or if the rate of interest
set for the forthcoming year looks attractive, keep them
invested.

Fixed interest security Investment involving a rate of interest
that is known when the investment is made and which is
guaranteed not to change within a set future period. Such a
security is either a bond that is issued by the Government (e.g.
a gilt), by a company (e.g. a corporate bond) or by some other
institution.

Flat fee Pre-stated and fixed charge made by financial adviser
for financial advice.

**Free Standing Additional Voluntary Contributions
(FSAVs)** These are like AVCs (above), save that they are not
paid into an existing occupational pension but into another
top-up pension that is quite separately purchased from an
insurance company.

FTSE 100 The London stock market index. The share price
values of the 100 largest British companies are used to calculate
it. The returns and maturity values of some investments are
sometimes contingent on the FTSE 100 achieving certain
pre-set performance targets by the time these payments become
due.

Fund Collective form of investment, such as a unit trust or
open-ended investment company.

Fund of funds Even more collective investment. Many
providers' investments are grouped under one amalgamative
umbrella.

Gilts Bonds issued by the UK government. They are classified
according to the time they have left to run before their
redemption dates. 'Short-dated' gilts have less than five years to
redemption, 'medium-dated' ones from five to fifteen years and
'long-dated' ones more than fifteen years to run. 'Undated' gilts
have no fixed redemption date.

Growth (capital) Increase in the capital value of an investment over time.

Guaranteed income bonds (GIBs) Possible repository for a lump-sum investment that promises to pay a fixed level of annual income over five years or longer and then return the capital sum originally invested.

Guaranteed rates Rates of return guaranteed to be available during the whole of the lifespan of an investment.

High-yield bonds These involve investing in bonds which, in the words of Mark Colegate, are issued 'by companies that the market considers to have a greater chance of not being able to meet interest payments' and thus 'tend to have to offer higher interest payments to attract investors'. In City-speak 'high-yield' is a euphemism for 'junk', which more clearly denotes the degree of risk these bonds involve. Crucial to their managers' success in producing high yields (but not at the expense of much or any erosion of capital invested) is the expertise of these managers, which is often conspicuously evident amongst the investment arms of life insurance companies. Some experts believe that high-yield bond funds should be purchased for income only and not with any expectation of any capital growth; if this does (rather commendably) materialise, it should be regarded as a bonus. Capital erosion is often less likely if the experienced team managing a high-yield bond fund place part of it in equities or quasi-equities and into lower-risk corporate bonds.

Increasing annuities The payments these annuities provide increase either at a fixed rate each year or rise in line with inflation. Understandably, they start from rather low initial rates.

Inheritance Tax At present, you can leave an estate worth £242,000 before any Inheritance Tax is due, but for estates worth more than this, a liability on the surplus amount involves a hefty 40 per cent. Nothing left to a surviving spouse is subject to this tax, whose elimination or reduction should be part of your retirement planning and will-making. A Skandia Life sponsored guide to Inheritance Tax is available from Madison

Money Management, 44 High Street, Bagshot, Surrey GU19 5AP, Tel. 01276 453343.

Investment-linked annuities   As these are directly linked to stock market performance, they involve much higher risks than many other types of annuity, but could produce much higher income than their rivals.

Job Seeker's Allowance (JSA)   In effect, this payment combines income support with unemployment benefit. Available only for the first six months of unemployment and taxable, it consists of a contributions-based allowance that is available to those who have made Class One National Insurance contributions for a stipulated period, and also an income-related and means-tested further allowance, to which those who have left their jobs voluntarily or taken voluntary redundancy may not be eligible. If appropriate, you can apply for just the contributions-based allowance. Some points made in a Department of Social Security leaflet are worthy of the particular attention of early leavers. The first is that this allowance is for the unemployed who have not reached state pension age, are capable of working and are available for work, and actively seeking it. The second is that a statutory redundancy payment does not affect your JSA but this may not be paid straightaway if you take voluntary early retirement. The third is that receipt of an occupational or personal pension may reduce a JSA. Finally, those aged 60–4 who do not want to sign on at the Job Centre every two weeks can claim income support instead.

Joint life annuity   An option that a prospective annuitant who is married or has a partner may prefer. It involves the purchase, not of a single life annuity, but one that will continue paying an income to a spouse or partner after the annuitant's death. This advantage is offset by the fact that initially the joint life annuity will provide a lower income than would a single life arrangement. Naturally, this reduction depends on how much of your annuity income you want to continue after your death. This continuing income is commonly set at two-thirds or one-half of the level of income received by the annuitant at death.

Junk bonds   Bonds issued by companies with poor credit ratings or no credit history. *Caveat emptor!* (See high-yield bonds above.)

Level annuity   This pays the annuitant the same amount of income year after year. What this also offers is peace of mind, for these level payouts are guaranteed. The only downside involves the question of whether you can cope on an income that will remain static, possibly for very many years, during which many prices will rise.

Lump sum investment   (a) A process that will greatly and rightly preoccupy the early leaver who has part of all of a severance sum to invest so as to augment income and produce capital growth. (b) A term involving an investment in which, at one particular time and on a one-off basis you place a sizeable amount of money.

Market value adjustment (MVA)   Investors in With Profits bonds may want or may have to encash these at a time that is deemed inopportune by and for the insurance company that provided them, and potentially damaging to remaining investors. An example of such a time would be when the stock market is seriously depressed and so too are the underlying assets of the fund. The insurance company may apply an MVA which allows them, if they deem it appropriate, to repay an investor less than the current market value of the bonds held. However, historically an MVA has not often been applied and is not even written into the terms on which some With Profits bonds can be purchased. During any application of an MVA try, if possible, to defer encashment of your bonds until its removal. In general, the stronger the company's financial reserves, the less likelihood there is that an MVA will be applied.

Managed income funds   These involve an investment portfolio of both bonds and shares, as do UK equity and bond income funds. However, these managed funds can feature overseas investments.

Maxi ISA   A total of £7000 per annum can be invested in this untaxed savings product. All of this annual amount can involve stocks and shares, or a lesser stake in stocks and shares can be held in conjunction with either cash deposits to a maximum of £3000 and/or life insurance up to £1000. This makes the limits for the components of a maxi ISA quite flexible. If you want to invest more than £3000 in stocks and shares, and have this investment made tax-free because of its ISA wrapper, a maxi ISA is the product to go for.

Mini ISA   Tax-free annual investment of £5000. This involves £3000 being invested in stocks and shares, £1000 being placed in cash deposits and £1000 in life insurance. With mini ISAs the limits are fixed. This means that, even if you put nothing into, say, a cash mini ISA during a financial year, you could still only invest the maximum of £3000 into its stocks and shares component.

Money purchase scheme   Description of a private pension or company pension. In the latter, if the contributing employee leaves the company, what has accumulated through previous payments into this scheme may be left to grow until statutory retirement age is reached. Alternatively, the employee may sometimes (perhaps with some difficulty) be able to arrange to transfer this accumulation into the superannuation scheme of the next employer. When the term 'money purchase' refers to an individual's private pension, it has a more literal meaning in that the individual's own independent and sole contributions to the pension are all that underpin it.

National Savings   Government-backed organisation offering a range of savings plans that include guaranteed and tax-free returns which are practically risk-free. As Sarah Modlock has commented, they are the 'sparklers' rather than the 'rockets' of the savings world: they are safe, unlikely to burn your fingers and give a rather lacklustre performance that many market alternatives rather leave in the shade. Of most interest to the fully retired are Pensioner Bonds, a taxable, lump-sum investment that pays you monthly fixed-rate interest as income straight into a current or savings account. Some early leavers have (historically) been advised to look at Index-linked Savings Certificates. They provide a tax-free lump sum investment that moves in line with inflation and earns interest over a set term. There is a choice between a two-year and a five-year term, and up to £10,000 can be invested into each type without affecting any other tax-free investments you may have.

No-notice (instant access) account Savings account requiring no advance warning or notice before withdrawals can be made – on the spot, instantly or electronically via the telephone or Internet. Many such accounts do not penalise their holders for rapid access to their money by offering low interest rates.

Non-taxpayers' investments Non-taxpayers can receive interest on savings accounts gross, if form R85 (obtainable from banks, building societies and tax offices) is completed. These individuals can also reclaim any tax levied on bond-derived income from unit trusts that are held outside an ISA. As for gilts, non-taxpayers can apply to the Bank of England to have tax on income from these paid gross.

Occupational pensions Superannuation arrangements that involve employment. Sometimes these are known as 'works pensions' or 'company schemes'. Broadly, there are two types. The first – technically called 'defined contribution' or 'money purchase' pensions – involves contributions being invested on the stockmarket to create a pot of money at retirement. One possible drawback is that contributors risk poor returns from the investments chosen. The second type of company scheme (commonly available to many public-sector workers such as teachers) is the 'defined-benefit' or 'final-salary' scheme. On retirement an annual (often index-linked) pension is paid whose size depends on the number of years those involved have contributed. Many public-service employees wise enough throughout full careers to have remained in, and not to have transferred out of, final-salary schemes have found that, at statutory retirement age, their occupational pensions have paid them roughly two-thirds of their final salaries! A major advantage of occupational schemes is that the Inland Revenue provides tax relief on contributions that can represent as much as 15 per cent of annual earnings.

Paper investments Those not involving visible or tangible investments in such physical possessions as classic cars, fine wines or watercolour paintings. Most investments that are recommended to the early retired are paper investments, if not always paper tigers!

Pensioner Bonds   See National Savings.

Performance figures   Figures comparing the past performance of rival investments over both short and long stretches of the recent past provide some 'form' that may be of some use in finding tomorrow's 'winners'. However, because it is unlikely that the future will repeat the conditions and financial environments of the recent past that influenced these performances, you should not attach too much importance to figures about past performance, because these are only historical. That said, consistently impressive past performances can provide reassurance to the risk-averse and cautious investor.

Permanent Interest-Bearing Shares (PIBS)   Special shares issued by building societies that pay a fixed rate of interest but which have no wind-up date.

Personal Equity Plan (PEP)   Tax-free investment in stocks and shares that preceded the ISA. Money that may historically have been invested in PEPs has no bearing on how much can be invested in ISAs.

Personal pension   Truly self-explanatory term for a superannuation arrangement made by an individual over and above others involving the State pension or an occupational one. For the majority of workers, such an arrangement, made early in a working life, is virtually a prerequisite for their early retirement.

Phased retirement   This arrangement – also known as 'staggered vesting' – is designed for those with substantial retirement 'pots' of over £100,000. Such a considerable pension fund is transferred into a phased retirement plan, which is split into a large number of separate segments or clusters whose benefits can be taken separately – an arrangement which provides great flexibility.

Portfolio   The spread or assembly of different investments.

Pound-cost averaging   A way of drip-feeding money into the stock market in a bid to deal with volatility.

Premature exit   Encashment of an investment before its timescale has ended or its 'life' is over. This proceeding can be subject to a financial penalty and so is often best avoided. However, with some investments that are 'sinking ships', such action can be financially life-saving.

Premium   (a) The annual amount of money paid for an insurance policy or loan. (b) Extra amount by which shares (or 'tangibles' such as some scarce and desirable cars) are selling above their established value.

Ratings   Some financial advisers, such as the David Aaron Partnership, express in terms of ratings their evaluation and assessment of the various risks of investing in different types of products, policies, plans, and schemes. These ratings are an invaluable way of rapidly determining how safe capital is likely to be if placed in a particular type of investment.

Real return   Actual return on investment, once the effect of inflation has been taken into account.

Reckonable service   Years of past employment that have featured payments into a pension scheme and so count in the final 'reckoning' or calculation on retirement of what value of pension this entitles the contributor to receive.

Redemption   Situation whereby a share or bond is bought back by the issuer.

Redemption yield   This has been best expressed by financial adviser, Graham Bates, as 'the annualised return on a fixed interest bond, taking into account any capital loss or gain that will be made if you hold the bond to maturity'.

Self-invested personal pension   Sophisticated and flexible arrangement available to those who can (and are allowed to) contribute at least £15,000 per annum to their own private pension arrangements.

Set-up fee   Charge an investor pays to have an investment set up in his or her name. Placing investments through brokers can often reduce this fee.

Split capital investment trust   A fixed-term investment offering a selection of classes of share, each with different rights to the trust's assets. The split can be two-way – between capital shares and income ones, the former receiving the income generated and the latter being the repository for the capital growth this investment produces. Split capital investment trusts can offer a higher income return.

Stakeholder pension   Low-cost, transparent and flexible pension product sold by insurance companies that is also available to non-earners. Young workers earning less than £30,000 a year may find this recently-launched product a much more attractive way of doing some extra saving for retirement (up to £3600 a year alongside a company pension) than involving themselves in the traditional occupational pension top-up that AVCs provide. This is because AVCs, unlike stakeholder arrangements, do not allow contributors on retirement to take 25 per cent of their fund as tax-free cash. AVCs are much better suited to those earning more than £30,000 a year who are ineligible for stakeholder arrangements.

Tax-efficient   Description of an investment meaning that whilst not tax-free, the investment is tax 'advantageous' because it involves low tax rates, given the tax-paying status, circumstances or legitimate strategies of the investor.

Term   Period during which an investment is held – its 'lifespan'.

Unit trust   Collective investment vehicle divided into units, which are bought at one price and profitably sold back to the fund manager at a later, higher one. Most usefully, a unit trust allows investors to make large 'pooled' investments in a fund that holds around 40 different stocks and shares, so cutting their costs and spreading the risks they take. Additionally, because the fund is a trust, each person's investment is protected. The structure of a unit trust is such that any falls in the value of a single share should be diluted, so investors face far less volatility than they would if they invested directly into shares. As the unit trust fund increases in value, the price of its units, which is quoted on the stock market, also grows. Unit trusts can represent an efficient way of investing in smaller companies and commodities and in overseas stockmarkets (which may be useful to complement and offset holdings on the UK one). In general, they are well-regulated holdings that are easy to buy and sell. If income is paid out, it is paid with a 'tax-credit' of 10 per cent, which cannot be reclaimed by non-taxpayers. Any capital gain made when units are sold is, if of appropriate size, subject to Capital Gains Tax. If, however, a unit trust can be purchased in an ISA 'wrapper', any income or growth you enjoy can be tax-exempt. As financial adviser Graham Bates has succinctly warned, 'if a unit trust is mostly using shares to provide income, it is important to be prepared for the fact that your income is likely to fluctuate'. One wise response to this drawback is 'to introduce some corporate bond funds into your portfolio to add some stability'.

Variable rate   Rate of interest that is not fixed but fluctuates over time.

Visible investments   Non-paper investments in 'tangibles' such as classic cars and fine wines.

Volatility   Characteristic of an investment whereby, over time, it is subject to major rises and falls in its value.

With-profit bonds   Bonds bought with lump sums that give access to a life insurance company's substantial with-profits fund. Commonly, such bonds are a five-year investment, which is often resorted to by income- or growth-seeking early leavers. These bonds represent yet another stock market investment but with the crucial difference that the insurance company in question tries to smooth out the inevitable ups and downs to which returns in the stock market are always subject by meting out investment returns as annual bonuses, holding back some of the profits in a good year to offset losses in a bad one.

Yield   Annual income produced by an investment, expressed as a percentage of its capital value.

Zero dividend preference shares (Zeros for short)   These are shares issued by a split capital investment trust that pay no income but produce a fixed capital gain at redemption, provided the fund meets certain conservative growth targets (which no previous zero has failed to meet). Zeros are a fixed-interest investment whose term is often five or six years. The best way of investing in a Zero is via an ISA unit trust. Many investors see such a holding as a useful further income source and, as such, it has appealed to the early retired in that the profits from Zeros are treated as capital gains and so are an ideal means of soaking up the annual £7500 Capital Gains Tax exemption. In effect, this annual CGT allowance is used to take an income. As Piers Currie has put it, 'the income-free status lets many private investors realise their annual CGT allowance of Zeros at low risk'. Moreover, Zeros may further appeal to early-retired investors because they allow future expenditure that can be anticipated – on, say, a new car or a grown-up child's wedding – to be taken care of. Unlike normal shares, which you hope will appreciate in value as well as pay a regular dividend, Zeros pay a predetermined capital sum at a fixed date. As Helen Morris has pointed out, 'each Zero has an annual growth rate that accumulates into a fund repayment value that is realised when the trust reaches its wind-up date. The prospective return on a zero is a compound annual growth rate called the redemption yield.' It should finally be noted that Zeros are particularly attractive to higher-rate tax-payers.

Further reading

Anderson, A. and Peyre, R., *Managing Your Money*, The Investor's Portfolio, 1999.

Anderson, A. and Slaughter, J., *Investing for Income*, The Investor's Portfolio, 1995.

Anderson, R. and Dibben, M., *An Introduction to Investment*, The Investor's Portfolio, 6th edition, 1999.

Barr, A. and R., *Which Way to Buy, Sell and Move House*, Which Books, 1993.

Bean, Tadd and Wright, *Retirement Planning Guide*, Longman, 1991.

Bolles, R. N., *What Colour Is Your Parachute*, Ten Speed Press, 2000.

Consumers' Association, *Which Way to Save and Invest*, Hodder and Stoughton, 1995.

Consumers' Association, *You and Your Pension*, Hodder and Stoughton, 1990.

Galzen and Plumbley, *Changing Your Job After 35*, Telegraph Books, 1995.

Gray, H., *How to Enjoy Your Retirement*, Northcote House, 1987.

Scase, R., *Fit and Fifty*, Economic and Social Research Council, 2000.

Slater, J., *Investment Made Easy*, Orion, 1994.

Stone, M., *How to Choose a Personal Pension*, Commercial Union.

Towry Law, *Guide to Early Retirement*, 1998.

Walkington, L., *A Consumer's Guide to Lump Sum Investment*, Kogan Page, 1993.

Index